Be

BECOME YOUR TRUE SELF, AND INSPIRE THOSE AROUND YOU.

BAHRIYE GOREN-GULEK

T0307510

Published by
LID Publishing Inc.
31 West 34th Street, 8th Floor, Suite 8004, New York, NY 10001, US

One Adam Street, London. WC2N 6LE

info@lidpublishing.com
www.lidpublishing.com

A member of:
BPR
Business Publishers Roundtable

www.businesspublishersroundtable.com

All rights reserved. Without limiting the rights under copyright reserved, no part of this publication may be reproduced, stored or introduced into a retrieval system, or transmitted, in any form or by any means (electronic, mechanical, photocopying, recording or otherwise) without the prior written permission of both the copyright owners and the publisher of this book.

© Bahriye Goren-Gulek 2016
© LID Publishing Inc. 2016

Printed in the United States
ISBN: 978-0-9860793-2-0

Page design: Caroline Li & Sara Taheri

Be

BECOME YOUR TRUE SELF, AND INSPIRE THOSE AROUND YOU.

BAHRIYE GOREN-GULEK

LID

LONDON
MADRID
MEXICO CITY
NEW YORK
BARCELONA
MONTERREY
SHANGHAI
BOGOTA
BUENOS AIRES
SAN FRANCISCO

This book is dedicated to:

My husband Tan
My son Hugo
& My parents

Thank you for being the light of my life

Table of Contents

Acknowledgements

I would like to thank the many people who helped me write this book. Over the course of the past years, I have been talking to many friends, colleagues, clients, and family members, to crystalize the concepts that I had in my head for the book.

First, I want to thank my husband Tan Gulek, who encouraged me on those days where I had a writer's block to keep going. He pushed me on numerous occasions to continue believing in this book, to put my ego and fears aside and keep on writing. Not to mention the number of discussions we've had at home about the various chapters, where he always managed to challenge me to bring each chapter to a higher level.

I also want to thank my mother, Adriana, as she was the one who told me when I was a little girl, how much she loves my writing style and I should do something with it. She always told me I could do anything I set my mind to, including becoming an author.

I would like to thank the people I interviewed for this book, who brought each concept to life, by sharing their personal stories: Emile de Beer, Bernard Kreilmann, Heleen Westerhuijs-Marinelli, Manfred Aben, Jennifer Barckley, Anita Keij, John Tanner and Sarah Miller.

I would like to thank LID publishing and the whole team that worked hard to make this book happen, especially my editor Sara Taheri, Caroline Li and Andrew Mueller, who have been involved from up close.

Last but not least: it would be impossible to list all the names of the people who have inspired me and have been there for me the past years, but I would still like to thank each and every one of you.

Chapter 1:
Intuition

"The quieter
you become,
the more you
can hear."

Ram Dass, spiritual teacher and author

Intuition is defined as the ability to understand something instinctively, without the need for conscious reasoning. Carl Jung, Swiss psychiatrist and psychotherapist, described intuition as perception via the unconscious that brings forth ideas, images, new possibilities, and ways out of blocked situations.

We tend to say: "I have a hunch", or "I have a gut feeling" when there is something we *know* even though we cannot rationally explain why we have that strong sense of inner knowing. Even though we are all familiar with those moments, most of us don't know what to do with it, let alone trust it.

Nobody really seems to understand where this inner knowledge comes from, how to recognize it, or how to cultivate it. Yet over the years it has become very clear to me that the best leaders have this rare natural ability to tune into their intuition, instinctively, and they're not scared of trusting it. Quite the contrary; they take it as one of the key inputs for decision-making. An internal compass if you will. And, needless to say, it takes intuition to spark creativity and innovation. Novel ideas emerge from a creative source, which is yet to be defined scientifically.

Possibly the closest thing to a scientific explanation is described by Dr Daniel J Siegel, a clinical professor of psychiatry at the UCLA (University of California, Los Angeles) School of Medicine. Based on his research, he describes intuition as "being in touch with the wisdom of the body". According to Siegel, the right hemisphere of our prefrontal cortex receives information from the body, including our heart and intestines (gut), and uses this input to give us a 'gut feeling'. An inexplicable experience of 'that little voice' informs us in a non-rational way which actions to take. Siegel makes the distinction between wise decisions versus logical ones. The first one being the result of an integrated functioning of both the left and right side of the brain, versus the logical decisions, which are based primarily on a rational way of thinking, informed and dominated by parts located in the left side of the brain. And even though recent research from the university of Utah, led by neuroscientist Dr. Jeff Anderson, is debunking the myth of people being more right- versus left-sided thinkers and personalities, Dr Jeff Anderson is also stating that, "It's absolutely true that some brain functions occur in one or the other side of the brain. Language tends to be on the left; attention or mindfulness, more on the right."

The point is that our current society – especially the corporate world, as well as the academic world – is set up in a way that we are evaluated, valued, and rewarded based on our analytical, rational performance. This was also beautifully explained by Sir Ken Robinson in his famous Ted Talk 'Do schools kill creativity? It starts all the way back in primary school and continues through high school and onwards. At the top of the list of priority courses we have mathematics and languages. You are seen as 'smart' only when you are good at either one, or both, of these. This trend is continued after graduation, when we start working and parenting, etc.

So unless you are an artist, poet, or dancer, it's just not acceptable to tell people in a professional environment: "Do what feels right from the gut. Be mindful!"

Both leaders and employees are looking for something more tangible to hold on to. And yet we feel confined and chained when we are bound to rules and structure that don't stimulate the joy and space needed for optimal motivation, productivity, and creativity.

While recent studies are showing the positive effects of mindfulness on an individual's performance, there is still very little data on the effects of a leader's mindfulness on the happiness and productivity of their teams. Based on my experience with senior-level executive clients as well as my own background, I know the immense effects a mindful leader can have on the people around him, if he is fully observant to what is going on, right now, within himself and the people around him. If he is alert and *aware* of what he is thinking *and* feeling, and acts based on both intuition and rational reasoning, then he will have a profoundly stronger and more positive impact on his team. In other words: if we, as leaders, observe our own thought processes and feelings before we respond to what people around us are doing, I can guarantee a more effective and joyful work place for both the leader and the team.

In the 2014 article by Jochen Reb, Jayanth Narayanan, and Sankalp Chaturvedi published in the *Mindfulness Journal*, "Leading Mindfully: Two Studies of the Influence of Supervisor Trait Mindfulness on Employee Well-Being and Performance", we can actually start drawing some tentative scientific conclusions that confirm the above. Although further research with more data points and more diverse samples is needed, the results from this study start suggesting that the quality of attention and awareness that a leader possesses may actually have a direct impact on those she or he supervises. These results also fit well within broader mindfulness literature, suggesting that mindfulness improves social relationships through improved communication and an increase in empathic concern towards others. Mindfulness helps us build deeper connections. Deeper connections make us feel more inspired.

Intuition can be cultivated through the practice of mindfulness. Have you ever wondered why we are called 'human beings' instead of 'human thinkers' or 'human doers'? It is good to allow ourselves to just sit still and be in a state of effortless being for a little while every day in the early mornings; more so if you have a busy day ahead, and around sunset to connect to our inner wisdom through silence. By focusing on being, we get more and more in tune with our inner voice, with who we truly are. But before we get to how we can do this and tune into this source of intuition, it is worthwhile to understand how we 'lost' it. Because in the end, our natural state is one where we are connecting both sides of our brains and are mindful throughout the day, without it being a conscious effort.

Just look at a child playing outside, and you will understand what I mean. When did we lose the ability to be mindful naturally, to be in the moment, in tune with who we really are? This is where our thought process and our stories come into play.

The stories we tell ourselves

As human beings we are known to be notorious storytellers. Our whole life experience is based on the stories we tell ourselves. Think about it. Isn't every experience you recall a personal commentary, a thought, a perception, even an interpretation of occurrences? Two people can attend the exact same concert yet have two completely different thoughts about it and, as a result, two totally different stories to tell afterwards. You probably describe the last company outing very differently than some of your colleagues or team members might describe it. And what happens when we add the opinions and expectations of people around us to our own thoughts? The mixture of all these thoughts and opinions becomes our story and description of who we are, or who we *think* we are.

Our thoughts create our stories, which in turn create our life – or rather, it creates how we *experience* our life.

In essence, our characters and personalities are a result of the stories we create about ourselves, as well as the people that influence us, especially at a younger age. I don't want to go too deeply into this as it could be a topic for a separate book, but the ancient Chinese philosopher Lao Tzu summed it up perfectly when he wrote: "Watch your thoughts; they become words. Watch your words; they become actions. Watch your actions; they become habits. Watch your habits; they become character. Watch your character; it becomes your destiny."

The thoughts and words Lao Tzu refers to are literally the stories we tell ourselves and others, over and over again.

So then, how exactly does this relate to intuition?

In essence: our fears and desires are a direct result of the stories we tell ourselves, and in turn these stories reinforce our fears and desires, and the vicious cycle begins. As a child, you weren't scared to speak your mind. And yet, over time, you got conditioned to sometimes bite your tongue. You might have been humiliated (or felt humiliated) when you spoke up and people reacted adversely, so the story you told yourself was that when you speak up in certain situations, you get 'punished', which turned you somewhat introverted. As David Lynch (director and screenwriter) pointed out so eloquently: "We think we understand the rules when we become adults but what we really experience is a narrowing of the imagination."

This same principle applies to the workplace. I've worked in environments where people are governed by fear. And guess what? Most likely, the leaders in those workplaces have many fears within themselves. We all know the insecure overachiever profile. I was even recruited by one of my first employers because I was one of them. But when an insecure overachiever gets to be in charge, they will demand the same work ethic from the people who work for them. I can guarantee you fear is never the best adviser.

The first time I became a leader, I wasn't leading with awareness at all, and it was reflected in how my team was operating. I didn't realize a lot of my words and actions were driven by my own insecurities, and it resulted in my team behaving in the same way. Fear makes people shut down, and nothing is more detrimental to creativity than fear.

The point here is clear: people around us mirror who we are and what we radiate. If we are mindful and at peace, the people we lead will become more mindful and more at peace. Professor Mark Beeman, who specializes in cognitive neuroscience at Northwestern University, has conducted one of the most groundbreaking studies on insights and where creative problem-solving comes from. He has shown different patterns of brain activity in high-insight versus low-insight anagram solvers, when people are completely at rest. The key conclusion was that insights do not come from logical reasoning, but are a sudden knowing that pops up in a restful state. They emerge out of a moment of nothingness. They emerge from what I would call intuition.

So how do we tune into this magical source called intuition? It is actually simpler than you might think, yet at the same time, its simplicity is also one of the hardest things to achieve, especially in our digitally 'always on' society.

First of all, it's important to realize that your intuition is already present. It's inside of you, so you don't need to go anywhere or do anything! I have participated in many corporate and self-help training programmes out there, seeking tools to become a better person. Drumming sessions to build better teams and drum out the frustrations? Why not? Phrases like 'limiting beliefs' and 'growing edge' are thrown at you from all directions. I've seen colleagues break down, weeping, in some of these workshops, because they feel lost.

It was only after I took a break from going to these workshops that I could see what the main learning point was. The key is to *remove the barriers* we have put in place, versus searching to find that holy grail as if it is something *outside* of us. Over the years, we have become so skilled at protecting ourselves, our image, our status, that in the process we have also killed that which makes us the best leaders: our inner wisdom. We have become externally driven versus internally driven. You must recall those moments where you feel this tinkling in your gut. When all of a sudden you get an idea, or you are interviewing someone for a job and you *know* that it's a bull's eye. You just know it!

So how to bring back what we seem to have lost?

You get your intuition back when you make space for it, when you are able to silence the mind. The word 'mindfulness' has become extremely popular these days, giving it both a mystical as well as an unreachable status. Nothing could be further from the truth. It basically comes down to being able to stop thinking, stop talking, stop doing, and listen. Still the rational mind. The mind that society has put on a pedestal, where we think we can outsmart life. But the fact of the matter is that the rational mind doesn't know everything. And, often, it can hinder us to find the right answers.

I challenge you to take 10-15 minutes of silence every day. Alone. Just switch off your phone, your laptop. And don't switch on the TV or radio either. Sit still, even if it feels uncomfortable or boring at first, close your eyes and just focus on your breath. If you are having a hard time sitting still, you can also take a walk while doing this. The key is to not interact, not think back over things that happened or things that you want to do. Just be. Of course, thoughts will come up. Let them. Don't resist. Just keep being still, whether by sitting still or while in motion. Be still.

Case study: Intuition in stillness

An interview with Emile de Beer, founder of SilverRed, Dubai

When I was thinking about who to interview for the topic of intuition and leadership, one person directly came to mind: Emile de Beer, founder of SilverRed. SilverRed supplies and customizes work-wear for companies in the oil and gas industry, petrochemical industry, steel industry or any other environment that requires work-wear with quality fabrics, good designs, and extreme comfort.

Why? Because Emile did something quite remarkable: he started a (by now) multi-million-dollar company single-handedly in Dubai after following his 'gut' or intuition, that told him he had to do it.

In my opinion, he is the embodiment of intuition-led leadership with awareness. Emile is one of those people with a very special kind of spark in their eyes, and since I met him, I've been trying to understand what the source of that spark is.

Emile is based in Dubai, in the United Arab Emirates, so we conducted our interview over the phone. It was early evening for Emile and the crack of dawn for me, as we have a ten-hour time difference. As it was the middle of the summer, it was a staggering 110 degrees Fahrenheit on Emile's side of the world, with a humidity averaging over 90%, which made me gain a newfound appreciation for the comparatively mildly sticky summers in New York. Emile and I have known each other for years, and we have a history of spending hours discussing anything from the meaning of life, to what to do when we retire. I was excited to get his viewpoint on the concept of intuition.

Emile, can you please tell us a little bit about your background and how you ended up where you are now?

Sure. I grew up in the town of Rotterdam in the Netherlands, raised by my French mother and Dutch father. I come from a family of four, three boys and one girl. Music is in our blood and I've been educated both as a professional violin player as well as a business economist, though I've been an entrepreneur for as long as I can remember.

While in college I started a few companies, and after college I started working for a company that specialized in safety clothing. In 2007 I gathered my courage to pack my bag (literally one bag!) and left for Dubai to start my own company, SilverRed. We focus on designing, manufacturing, and distributing work-wear that is comfortable, well-designed, and most importantly, creates a safer work environment.

Now my company is big enough and complex enough for me to have a team of talented people around me to help manage and further grow the business. I'm still the managing director and I oversee all major accounts and business development.

What do you do when you don't work?

To me, my family – which includes my wife and two kids – are my main priority and joy in life. After work, I love to come home, put the kids to bed, and enjoy a nice meal with my wife. I enjoy kitesurfing and just love nature in general. And stillness. The very early hours in the day are especially sacred to me. While everyone is still asleep, I get up and enjoy that time of day, just before dawn. It's the perfect time to be still. I enjoy the stillness. It helps me gather my thoughts but, most importantly, it helps me connect to my core, to my intuition. That little voice we all have inside but gets drowned out by the noise of everyday hustle and bustle.

I will ask about that connection with your intuition in a while, but can you please tell us a little about how you found the courage to start SilverRed?

SilverRed really was a calling. It wasn't so much a rational decision as a 'knowing' I had deep inside that it was something I just had to do, as strange as that may sound. From the very start, SilverRed didn't feel like a project or assignment. It didn't feel like something I should fear either. It actually felt like a path, if that makes sense. It felt like a path without a specific goal, but with a clear vision. But the path in and of itself felt like the goal.

I did have a business plan, of course. And I spent a lot of time on it. But the finances or business results were not my main focus in the beginning. Instead, I was focused on getting that first client and making sure I delivered and over-delivered for that client. Then one client turned into two clients, turned into three, etc. And each time, the clients turned into bigger accounts. Before I knew it, I had to look in more detail at the whole financial picture, as projections started to matter. But that was only after I fully let myself be guided by my intuition; then I stayed focused on the path without thinking too much about the outcome.

Now we're in a place where we are growing at least double digits year on year, and companies are calling *us* instead of us chasing them, based on what they see on our website or from what they've heard from people in the industry. It really all happened without me purposefully being too focused on the outcome, but rather by tuning into my intuition or inner voice along the way, and staying true to that inner voice.

So let's go back to what you said earlier about intuition, about that inner voice, and finding ways to connect to it.

Well, as I mentioned earlier, making the decision to start SilverRed was a direct outcome of listening to my intuition. I had to do it. And knowing I had to do it came out of a moment of stillness. It came from the stillness of my mind. It came out of 'nothingness'. Once, I literally even had an image or vision, seeing myself walking in the desert with an enormous feeling of power and strength. And that was when I was still living in the Netherlands. Based on my intuition, I quit my job and really had trust, deep inside. But it didn't happen overnight. After I quit my job, I had a full year where I wasn't working. I was preparing for all this, even though from the outside it looked as though I was doing nothing. But it was from that phase of doing 'nothing' that my true path emerged.

Even though things have been stressful at times, I purposefully let things flow. And I continued to trust. I completely trusted my intuition on this venture. I think that has been core to my success. I kept trusting even though things were not always under my control. Control over the numbers or business results. Control over whether a potential client would say yes. But really giving it my full 100% and trusting that business would come if I continued giving it my all with a concept I truly believed in. Of course, the phase of following your intuition, without looking too much at the numbers and results, lessens once business starts growing. Now I feel I have more of a balance. Intuition is important, yes, but so is day-to-day management, the reality that comes with growing a business and serving clients, and making sure you always deliver. Now I have more focus on numbers, agreements, and exercising control. Much more than when I first started. But that's necessary.

What always remains is that feeling of trust. Trusting that you are making the right decisions and you are on the right path.

Again, moments of silence are crucial. Vacation time is crucial. It's very important to disconnect, so you are better able to perform at your best when you do connect.

Weekends are sacred to me. Unless it is really necessary, I choose not to work at weekends. My family and my wife are very important to me to recharge. I cannot work 24/7 and, quite frankly, it's really not something I want to do.

My home and my family are my sanctuary. As I mentioned, half an hour to an hour at the crack of dawn is very important to stay connected with my intuition.

The thing that's tricky about intuition is when you are on a running train. Perhaps if you've been in the same job or career for the past decade, it can become very hard to really identify something as your intuition. It is hard to break free from a path like that. How do you know that something (a thought or a feeling) is your intuition? Often, you can clearly see it in hindsight, but in those moments where you feel this hunch, it's very hard to know it for sure because we tend to over-think and over-rationalize things.

So when does that switch from a hunch to actually knowing what it is? And what do you need to do about it? You tell me. That is something everyone has to try for him or herself. I can now see the consequences of my intuition from back then. But how difficult is it to follow your intuition daily? I think the key really remains to continuously connect to that inner silence. Your intuition is always within you, but you need to find a way to access it. And that way is through silence. It is by being in a flow and feeling freedom. It is hard to connect to intuition when you are tied down.

Suppose you are in a job or in a situation that is not true to who you are. You often feel very strongly that something isn't right. You may even feel what it is you need to do. But we often push those feelings away because we feel as though there is no way out. Just look at people around you who are in unhappy relationships. The ones who dare to break free – yes, they will have a moment of deep fear and mourning, but shortly afterwards often comes a period of immense strength and freedom. And that always takes you somewhere better.

It's important to have a vision, but it's equally important along the way to learn to let go of control. Yes, it's scary, but the rewards are much higher.

So where will you go from here?

Well, I can imagine in a few years I might sell the business, which will mean I can focus my energy on something else. I will do another deep dive into my intuition. I'm pretty sure SilverRed is not my last endeavour, and the thought of doing something completely different in a few years excites me a lot. I think sticking to one industry or career is something society has imprinted on us, but I'm not sure it has been for the benefit of most people.

Chapter 2:
Vision

"If you don't know where you are going, any road will lead you there."

Lewis Carroll, author

Have you ever noticed how many of us are running after goals that are driven by society, by what is expected, by what we think defines success, by how we want to be viewed by our co-workers, our friends, our family, even by strangers? "Oh, let's go for the next title up, buy a bigger house, a bigger diamond. Oh, and look at what my former classmates have achieved already. I want that, too!"

What if we were to look within instead? What if we were to create a personal vision, whispered in silence in our ear when we are truly still, and base our intentions, thoughts, and actions on what our heart tells us? What if we were to become our true selves? It all spirals into such a beautiful journey when you start living your life inside out, versus the other way around. Carl Jung was one of those brilliant scholars able to put this into words in a simple yet profound way: "Who looks outside dreams. Who looks inside, awakens."

As a brand strategist, my main objective in any project I work on is to help companies and brands define their purpose. As a lecturer at a business school, my main objective is to empower my students to be their best selves and become inspiring leaders of the future. The key to becoming that is by holding a clear personal vision. I always ask them: why would people want to align themselves with you or your company's beliefs? This is where a sense of purpose comes in.

Purpose doesn't have to be altruistic or philanthropic in nature. A purpose is something you believe in, something you stand for, that 'thing' that makes you different from the competition, even if you are offering the exact same product or service. A purpose defines how your actions serve others and contribute to the world. Whether that is challenging the status quo in the case of (the old) Apple, or producing food with integrity in the case of Chipotle Mexican Grill; as long as you have a vision of what you want your world to look like in an ideal scenario, then that is your purpose.

Simon Sinek, author, speaker, and consultant on leadership and management worded it perfectly when he stated: "People don't buy *what* you do, they buy *why* you do it. There are leaders and those who lead. Leaders hold a place of authority, while those that lead inspire."

So how to bring this down to a practical level when you are heading a team, or running a company, or when you are trying to raise three happy kids?

The key is to have a *personal* vision built on authentic intentions, driven by your heart's purpose that you have articulated clearly for yourself. That's quite a mouthful, and I know what you are thinking: "That's easier said than done! I have no idea what my heart's purpose is."

Let me explain what I mean. I remember vividly when I started as a young graduate trainee at Unilever; there was one key slogan that was used internally at all times: "Begin with the end in mind." I would hear this sentence in every meeting, every evaluation, even during lunch. It's one of the key concepts that Stephen Covey discusses in his book *The Seven Habits of Highly Effective People*. It's important to hold a clear image of where you want to be. Where you want your road to lead to, and only thereafter take purposeful action to bring that image to life.

The question you want to ask yourself first and foremost is: Who am I? That question might sound too philosophical, but it really is a very important question to ask yourself. Who are you really, deep down? Not who your parents wanted you to be, or how you want to be viewed in the world. But underneath all those layers, who is there?

On a day-to-day basis, are you doing what you really want to do? It is important to be brutally honest with yourself. There is no right or wrong answer, and you don't even have to admit it to anyone but yourself. Perhaps you have become who you *thought* you wanted to be, or maybe who you were *expected* to be, but that achievement has come at the expense of things that could have made you much happier.

"Who am I?" is a tough question to answer, because it actually means you need to figure out what you really want. Only when you become fully aware of your desires will you understand who is beneath all those layers that society puts on us.

Sadly, most people run on autopilot and they don't know what they want. People are too busy working for their next pay cheque and rushing home to pick up the kids or prepare dinner. Who has time to think these things through or, better yet, not think and become aware by taking the time to be still?

What is a little easier to achieve is realizing what we don't want. And that is already a great starting point. Eliminating the things that don't spark your soul is a great way to find out what you do want.

Sometimes you have to close one door in order for another door to open. But that takes a lot of courage, especially when you don't know when that new door will appear, let alone open. This is where trust and intuition come in.

Trust your intuition.

When you are truly unhappy in a given situation, it is imperative to take action, and not let years pass by.

Once you are clear on what you do NOT want, then the next step becomes finding your heart's true purpose. In other words: *"What makes you tick?"*

A tool you can use to identify what you want in life is to think back to your childhood. Which activities would make the hours pass by like minutes? Or made you feel like time stood still and you were fully in the moment?

Let me give you a personal example. When I was a child, I loved to play with children who were younger than me, and teach them things. I also loved to draw, daydream, and write short stories. It is no surprise to me that I ended up being a university lecturer, while at the same time working for a creative agency, and writing my book.

It took me a long time to find out what I love to do and then define my personal vision, which in my case is about bringing positive change to people's lives through communication and teaching. It doesn't matter what company I work for, or which university I teach at, because wherever I go, my personal vision remains the same. I can translate this vision to fit the specific context I am in at any given moment, to inspire those around me.

However, I only got to that vision after much trial and error. As I said earlier, it helps to first identify what you don't like. But then it's key to push yourself and tune into feeling where your heart gravitates towards. When you love what you do and you have a clear vision or personal purpose, you truly don't have to 'work' another day in your life because it doesn't feel like work any more. Instead, it feels like those hours you spent as a child, playing or drawing.

When you have a personal sense of direction that is close to your heart, the whole energy field around you changes. You speak with more conviction, you have more motivation; you are literally more inspiring to the people around you. And as we said earlier, the best leaders are the ones who inspire.

All of this is, of course, easier said than done.

Imagination is a key skill to have here. As the filmmaker James Cameron noted so truly: "Imagination is a force that can manifest a reality."

Literally, the definition of imagination is: “Having the ability to form new images and sensations in the mind that are not perceived through senses such as sight, hearing, or other senses.”

What you imagine and visualize in your mind with faith and emotion, more often than not comes into being. Thought energy is extremely powerful when followed by the right language and actions. But it all starts with the images we hold in our minds. If you don’t make a conscious effort to visualize who you are and what you want in life, then you give power to unconscious thoughts and circumstances to shape your life. That’s when you feel like your life is not in your own control, or, worse, you can feel like a victim if you cannot seem to achieve the things you would like to achieve in life.

Being a visionary is all about connecting with yourself, your true self, and then imagining how that can contribute in a positive way to the world around you. This way you can express yourself and feel fulfilled.

One of the most common and biggest mistakes is pursuing a career or a job because it pays better or because it’s more prestigious. You will always end up feeling drained and non-fulfilled if that is your primary motivation for doing what you are doing. And yet, most people are in that position. I will be discussing this further in chapter 7.

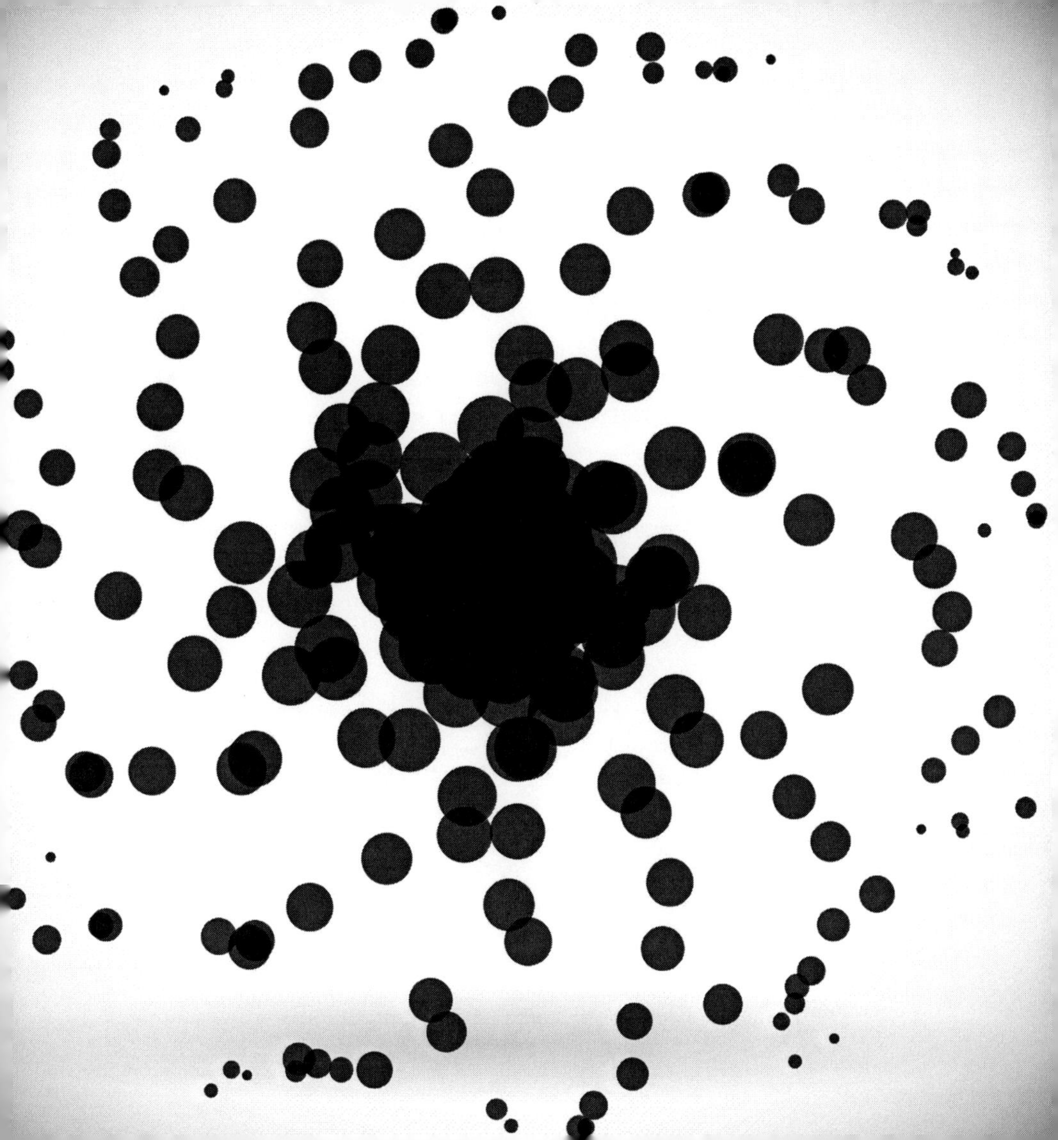

Bringing other people on board

As a leader, you have to move beyond your personal vision in order to inspire others and bring a group of people to the next level. You should always be clear on what the collective vision is. I call that the 'North Star'. The North Star is a vision that is set not only by you as the leader, but also by the people around you, together. In order for that to happen, you need to remain open to what might come your way and how you can influence it as well, as long as it is aligned with your personal vision.

For this to happen, it's very important to be clear about the intention at the basis of your vision. Our intentions are the 'why' behind our vision. Your vision is a certain end result that you are trying to achieve. But there is an underlying reason why you want to achieve it.

Let me illustrate this with an example. I used to have a girl in my team who had a clear goal to become a chief marketing officer. Let's call this girl Laura.

When I asked Laura why she wanted to become a CMO, she said she wanted to make an impact in the company and help it grow by tapping into consumer needs. To get to the deeper underlying motivation, I again questioned why that was important to her and why she wanted to do it so badly. After digging deeper for a little while longer, continuously asking the question "Why?" we uncovered that the true intention behind Laura striving to become a CMO was validation for who she was as a human being, by being in charge and being a successful businesswoman. We then worked to understand what in her definition defined being successful, and how she would feel validated in the context of our team. It turned out that becoming a CMO was not the only way to stay true to her intentions.

Once you help people define their underlying intentions, it quickly becomes clear that most of us are quite similar when it comes to what drives and motivates us. Even though I believe we are all unique and have our own talents we can bring to this world, I also believe that deep down we are wired in a very similar way, and we are all connected. It is impossible to hurt someone else without hurting yourself. And vice versa, when you put yourself in the service of others for the good of the world, you are doing yourself a very big favour in the process.

Case study: Vision

An interview with Bernard Kreilmann, former CEO of Ferrero USA

I was extremely honoured, but most of all excited, when Bernard Kreilmann agreed to an interview for *Be*. As the former CEO of Ferrero USA, for many years he has been chief of Nutella, a product that brings happiness to so many people on a daily basis. Ferrero was originally an Italian company, and I was excited to understand more about how the former CEO for the US market thinks about leadership.

I met Bernard at the beginning of spring in 2015. It was a very nice spring day and I drove down to Somerset, New Jersey, which was just over an hour's drive from my office in Manhattan. When I entered the building I couldn't help but grin from ear to ear, as I was greeted by a gigantic Nutella jar standing right by the entrance. I admit to being a not-so-secret Nutella addict, so you can imagine my excitement. Shortly thereafter, Bernard welcomed me with a warm hello into his office.

Bernard, how would you define good leadership?

Well, first of all, I think it's important to make the distinction between a leader and a mentor. A leader's role is to reach a goal with a team as a vehicle. A mentor is someone who guides and encourages, and makes sure people reach their own individual goals, which should complement each other, if done right. A good leader is usually also a mentor.

Good leaders are interested in building their success through the progress of the people they are leading. And they have fun with that. They love to see people grow, and feel responsible for them. Unfortunately, sometimes there is a lot of ego in leadership. But real leaders are not driven by their egos. They thrive on seeing other people succeed.

I was lucky to have had leaders that were also amazing mentors throughout my career. You need that to be able to grow. Mentors give you confidence. My mentors were amazing. When I was younger, and relatively early on in my career, my vision was rather short-sighted. But my mentor could see further than I did, and he could see what I could grow into. He could see my true potential. As human beings, we sometimes create resistance to our own potential. It was my mentor that looked beyond my own restrictions and helped me create an aspirational vision. Sometimes you can't see the forest for the trees.

True leaders will try to accomplish goals through their teams, and not through their own beliefs or agenda alone. It is important to focus on your own vision as a leader, but at the same time it is important to remain open to what people around you are saying. And adapt accordingly.

What kind of a leader do you see yourself as?

As I described earlier, I like to see myself as a blend of both a leader and a mentor. I've been in a position as a leader where I had to restructure, and I can tell you, restructuring is a tough job because of the decisions you have to make.

When things are good it is relatively easy to be in charge. But when times are tough the true leaders emerge.

For example, in my teams, we don't value individual success as much as we do the team's success. In the end I think each success is always a group effort.

How do you see your role as a leader, especially with regards to setting forth a vision?

Well, as a leader it is crucial to establish strong principles and work ethics. Your role is to set the right example, creating a company culture and operating model so people are clear on their roles, responsibilities, and accountabilities.

Success comes from the team effort. As the leader your job is to inspire people, harmonize, and integrate the different functions. But within each function you need your experts. These are the people that make things work. My VP of marketing, for example, is better at marketing than I am. But I synthesize everything and have the talent to see what his recommendations can mean for the future. I create and hold the vision. As the leader, I define the overall direction of the company; the North Star, as you call it. But I would not be able to create harmony if I tried to control every aspect or function. I leave that up to the experts.

Can you please explain a bit more about how you define the vision or 'North Star'? And how you get people to follow the same North Star?

First of all, you have to find your own purpose. For me it is having a challenge that has substance. I'm mostly interested in the trajectory. The specific goals are not as interesting to me as the road that leads up to them.

For example, I'd get a certain mandate from the headquarters in Europe. I would then decide how to manage it here in the US. I'd create clear lines and responsibilities so that the people here would feel ownership as well. I love the challenge of getting people geared to move in the same direction. Creating synthesis. Figuring out how to get there. Working together towards achieving greatness by building something that has a positive impact. The aspect of positive improvement is very important to me, no matter where I am. That is my personal vision, and I take it with me to every company and challenge.

So whether you are leading a small local company or are the CEO of a multinational, as a leader it is important to find your own purpose, first and foremost. You have to figure out what your passion is. That is what you will have fun with and be able to inspire others with, no matter what context you are in.

You have to keep growing as a leader, too. Keep reinventing yourself. I call that agility. It is important to know when to push and when to pull. Knowing when to fill the space and when to leave the space as it is. Knowing when to step aside.

It's also important to accept failure and not fear it. There is a power behind failure, because it is an opportunity for learning and growth. As a leader it is impossible to always play it safe. You have to learn to sometimes let go. Also let go of the notion that you are able to control everything. Control is merely a reflection of your beliefs.

When creating a vision, it is important to listen. Co-creating the company vision with your team is the best thing you can do.

Leadership is about energising people to go over and beyond their expertise and comfort zone by stepping it up, and helping them understand the 'why?' – How does it all connect with the overall purpose, and with his or her purpose? That way everyone will feel motivated.

The key traits I see for a good leader are: curiosity, listening skills, observation skills, and the ability to absorb and synthesize a lot of diverse information. You have to be a little stubborn too, especially when you see something that others don't see.

In fact, there's nothing more inspirational than seeing something that others don't see.

Chapter 3:
Surrendering

"What could be more insane than to create inner resistance to what already is? Say yes to life and see how life suddenly starts working for you rather than against you."

Eckhart Tolle, author

When you hear the word 'surrender', what is the very first thing you think about? I'm guessing it's probably something along the lines of defeat or giving up. Surrender is a tricky word. Most people associate the word with something negative, where you have lost in some shape or form to someone else. Our dictionaries don't help either, as according to the official meaning from the *Merriam-Webster Dictionary*, surrender is defined as: "To give (oneself) up to the power of another, especially as a prisoner."

As I was doing my research for this book and talking to many people across the globe, I noticed that this particular concept of surrender was the least liked by far. I would get responses like: "Surrender? Are you kidding me? That's basically saying it's good to give up." Or: "Surrender? Why would you include that as one of the key concepts for getting to awareness?" These reactions were definitely no surprise to me, and yet I would like to argue that it's probably one of the most important concepts described in this book, especially given the fact that it is the least obvious one.

Let me start off by saying: when I talk about surrender, I am *not* talking about defeat. My definition of surrender is acceptance and knowing when to let go of control, and to have *trust* on a deeper level. Surrender is a more profound version of *acceptance*. Surrender has a level of deep trust within, and trust is key when we talk about inspirational leadership.

Leaders are known to dislike the idea of surrender. I have to admit that I also used to see surrendering as 'giving up', or 'losing' to someone else, which isn't easy for someone who is extremely competitive. But that definition is a very different type of surrender, or rather, a different type of frequency altogether, where we see life as a battle; someone wins, someone loses, versus trying to look for win-win situations that create long-term balance.

Think about it; when you have a cold and you want to get better as quickly as possible, does it help to resist your cold and go on as if you are fine? Or is it better to accept you have a cold, crawl into bed and rest for a day or two? Which approach do you think will ensure a quicker recovery? That is what I mean when I talk about surrender. Being able to surrender to the moment and its accompanying circumstances will enable you to transform the situation into the direction of your desire much quicker and with greater ease.

Surrender is about more than acceptance alone. There is an element of peace and, most importantly, faith. In other words, having trust. Surrender is about admitting and being at peace with the fact that we cannot always be in control. It's actually getting out of the way and being alert to what is happening right now, while keeping genuine intentions in your heart. I know this sounds lofty, but once you start practising the art of surrendering, you will notice it is actually quite tangible and brings tangible results, just like in the example of how to deal with a cold. I will explain this in more detail in an example later on.

First I want to emphasise that feeling the need to exercise tight control over every aspect of your life is a sure way to guarantee a miserable life. Because, let's face it, that is a mission impossible. And yet most of us, especially if you were drawn to picking up this book, are something of a control freak. It's what (we think) makes us a success in life. And even though there is truth to that, long-term success is very much a balancing act between controlling and knowing when to let go of control. Imagine a parent that always wants to stay in full control over their child. That type of mindset will hurt both child and parent. The same applies to most things in life.

Furthermore, being happy is more important than being right. What does that have to do with anything, you might say? Well, when we *think* we know exactly what we want, and we are convinced we are right, we might be losing sight of what could truly make us happy. Because when you are in that state of mind you will not see any other opportunities that might arise. You are basically closed off to other possibilities. Possibilities you could not have imagined yourself.

In the end: control is an illusion.

We think we control many things, while in reality we often don't. We can control our actions and reactions, yes. And those will have an effect on our circumstances and the people around us, but to think we control things fully is an illusion.

And as a leader, the more we try to control the people around us, the more they actually become demotivated. There is a huge power to empowering people to make their own decisions with clarity of direction. Surrendering to feelings of non-control can be very liberating as a leader, versus being a micro-manager, which often can completely backfire.

Surrendering frees us from anger and fear. It can give us a clear idea of how to handle difficult situations and gives us a sense of inner peace. This comes instantly when you decide not to 'fight' or resist.

"Whatever you resist persists," said Carl Jung.

This truly is one of my all-time favourite quotes. The more energy you give to what you do not want, by being angry or by resisting its existence, the more it will remain in your face (or life). Your best shot at changing the situation is by first surrendering to what *is*.

A prime example of this is something I witnessed within a company. The company had some rocky times where the number of clients wasn't consistent every year or even every month. People in the company started getting fearful about losing their jobs and panic was spreading rapidly. I noticed two executives who had opposite responses to this.

Even though Executive A knew the urgency of the situation, he remained calm and exuded a sense of trust. Executive B, however, radiated a lot of stress and became short-fused. In fact, he was one of the main reasons why employees started panicking. They were thinking: "If Executive B is panicking, then something really bad must be happening!"

When Executive A realized that this dynamic was going on, he radiated an even greater sense of calm and trust. He had a complete sense of surrender; a sense of letting go of control and trusting that more clients would come soon. Surrender does not mean that you don't take any action. It means that you take action while accepting the *current state of affairs*, and working to change it to what you want it to be.

The key difference between the two executives was that Executive A was not in a state of resistance, rather he was accepting of it. Executive B, however, let fear get the better of him. He wanted to control the current situation, which was impossible, and this made him an ineffective leader at the time.

Surrendering is also not to be mistaken with laziness. It is anything but doing nothing and waiting for life to hand what you want on a silver platter. Quite the contrary! In Buddhism, surrendering is called 'compassionate action'. It is about starting from where you are, right now, in this very moment, rather than resisting the current moment. That will enable you to keep your mind and heart open to possibilities and ways to change the current situation, if that is what you are after. You could also see surrender as completely giving yourself to the current situation, to see what will come your way as you flow with life, rather than struggling upstream.

Surrendering literally means accepting what is, right here, right now. You can and should want a vision of how you want to transform certain circumstances (as discussed in chapter 2), but you can only do that in an effective way, once you first accept what is. And it is actually the opposite of the misconception of giving up. By accepting what is, you will be able to respond to what is happening in a more alert and effective way, rather than trying to control the situation, starting from a negative mindset.

Surrendering to what 'is' means that you are truly in the present moment versus always thinking about what you want next. Now you might ask yourself: why would I want to do that? To be successful in what I do, I have to be looking, thinking and planning for the future at all times. The good news is that living in the present moment, while planning for the future, does not need to be mutually exclusive. You can be accepting of the current moment, while planning for the future. In fact, when you are accepting of the now, you are in a calmer and better place, so you can actually plan better as well!

When you master the art of surrender, it means you are letting go of control enough so you can look at all elements in a given context, noting anything that might be keeping you from moving in the desired direction. You are open to new and alternative ways of thinking, versus your fixed way of thinking, and can allow deeper levels of wisdom to guide you in your next steps. We sometimes don't see what's right in front of us because we are so fixated on what we want (or think we want).

Let me explain this concept with another real-life example. Something I experienced in my professional life.

When I was in my late twenties I was convinced that I wanted to become a partner at the firm I was working for at the time. Even though I didn't like what I was doing on a daily basis, I thought becoming a partner would somehow validate who I am as a person. The desire was heavily ego driven, versus tuning in to who I truly am and want to be. Thoughts like "If I don't make it as a partner, I am a failure," were dominating and loud in my mind. I remember vividly the exact moment when I realized I was completely on the wrong path: we were working with a small team on one of our biggest clients. Five of us were on location regularly, as we were preparing for workshops and key presentations. The timelines were so short that we all worked around the clock, and the tension within the team started building up because of the fast pace of intense project deliverables.

Working until the wee hours of the night became the norm. I was so focused on what I thought I wanted, which was to become a partner, that I completely let myself get caught up in this crazy flow. We would sometimes have a meeting at 7am and continue preparing for the next day through to 10pm or 11pm.

One particular night was a turning point for me, however. It was 1.30am and the entire team had gathered in the project director's hotel room. I remember being so tired and unhappy that at one point during the meeting I realized I just had to surrender to those feelings versus continuing to fight them and go on like a workaholic, trying to deliver on the project. At that exact moment in time I *let go of control.* The minute I did that it felt like a weight had lifted off my shoulders. Instantly. More importantly, I felt like I was seeing more clearly. I looked around the room and I saw my teammates in the crazy mode that I was in myself just a few moments ago, as well as the past years. They were passionately debating a certain topic, though I could see the exhaustion on their faces. Each of them had a family with little kids waiting for them back home in New York City, and yet they were in this hotel room on location for the project. Each one of them was about ten years older than I was at the time, and all of a sudden I saw it very clearly: I didn't want to be like them in ten years. I wanted my life to look very differently. I wanted to be able to enjoy dinner at home with my family. Heck, I even wanted to have time to prepare a nice dinner at home, walk the dog, enjoy a nice glass of wine with my loved one after dinner, and play with my kids. I also wanted to work for something I truly cared about. The client I was there for was a major corporation, one with whom I had zero aligned values. That made my conclusion even stronger. I was in the wrong job, and for me to pursue the track of becoming partner was absolutely insane!

A few months later, after careful planning and consideration, I quit and started my own company. To this day, it was the best decision I made in my career and it was that moment of full and complete surrender that helped me get on the right path for me.

Surrendering is all about going with the flow of life versus swimming upstream. Think about the example above. If I had continued swimming upstream, who knows where I might be right now. I might have actually made it to partner and I would be spending more than 60-70 hours a week doing something I don't enjoy or love. It's safe to say that is a sure way to an unhappy, unfulfilled life. Or, if I had never made it to partner, I might have literally wasted years and years of my life chasing a goal that wasn't in line with my true intentions to begin with.

Instead, I am now happier, both personally and professionally, than I could ever have imagined.

Case study: Surrender to your true path

An interview with Heleen Marinelli-Westerhuijs, art historian

Finding the right person to interview for the concept of surrender was probably the toughest challenge when writing this book, because it is one of the most misunderstood concepts discussed. I knew that if anyone was to instantly understand what I meant by surrender, that person would be Heleen Marinelli-Westerhuijs, a dear friend who I highly respect both for who she is professionally as well as on a personal note. Heleen is an art historian and published author based in New York City. I was thrilled and delighted that she was willing to share her story and perspective with us in this interview.

When I called Heleen for our interview, she stepped out of her apartment so that, as she stated herself, she could let the answers "come naturally and instinctively" without over-analysing her responses. I heard her say a loud "Si!" as she answered her phone, because she was responding to her Italian husband at the same time that, yes, she would love risotto for dinner. I already knew that this interview would, yet again, be an interesting one.

Heleen, can you please tell us a little bit about how you ended up where you currently are?

It really all started with a three-day trip to New York City. This city has been, and still is, key to my life story. I was 22 years old when I first visited New York with my brother, and it truly was one of the most important trips of my life. When I set foot in Manhattan, I felt something I had never felt before in my life, and never even knew existed. As soon as I came here I grew and felt bigger than ever before. I could think things I didn't dare think of before. For instance, writing was one of them. I knew I had to be in here. And I knew it in a split second when I arrived.

Until that first trip, I wasn't even thinking of working or living in New York, but afterwards I knew I had to be here. I kept coming back to the city every three months, flying back and forth from Amsterdam. New York became sort of an addiction, for which I worked hours and hours straight in all kinds of jobs, securing the possibility to go back time and time again. I didn't look any further than my next trip. And I knew it was the right thing. Then things started happening. I started to meet people, who in hindsight were exactly the people I had to meet. For example, I met the former Dutch consul general, and he started telling me about a project to write a book about the Dutch history of New York. Again, I had this instant inkling that I was going to be part of that project. I was still studying art history at the time. To cut a long story short, that meeting led me to the person who offered to sponsor that book, and me. This made it possible for me to come to the US and New York on a work visa, and the rest is history. It led me to writing the book that I co-authored, called *Exploring Historic Dutch New York*.

I literally sat down in a cubicle and two years later the book was done. All the meetings and talking to people and actually making it happen took a lot of time and, of course, initiative. All in all, when I think back about what I was trying to pursue, it could have been rather nerve-wracking. But I knew I was doing the right thing. The point is it all happened as I was letting things flow. All the things I needed and, most importantly, the people that had to come into my life to make it happen, literally came to me as I was letting things happen, if that makes sense. They literally happened to me. In that period I was on my own a lot. And that also led to a lot of listening to myself.

I met my husband in New York, and right now we are delighted to have a baby on the way. My family and friends are central to my life, as is the work I do. My personal interest is living an organic life in New York. It's really not my thing to sit at a desk at 9am and finish work at 5pm. Work, life, and passion are intertwined for me.

I'm a historian who writes to bring a message out into the world. There has never been a distinction between my work and who I am in my personal life. The two always blend together, and I think that also has to do with my love for New York. New York *is* my personal interest.

How does this link to the concept of awareness and surrender?

I think it's very important to surrender to the flow that you are in, to recognize the power of listening to yourself, even if you hear different things to what you would expect. You could say intuition played a big role, but I actually think (feel) it was something bigger than that.

Bigger than that? Can you please explain what you mean?

Well, in my opinion, our intuition is within ourselves. It is the voice that tells you what to do. But this was more than a little voice inside. It was much more tangible. It starts with a little voice, yes. But then it manifests itself in reality. The little voice inside became actual words that I spoke to people. I started reaching out to people to set up lunches. Those lunches led to other meetings. It's a very focused and practical energy that I am talking about. That is what I call awareness. Awareness to me is something very tangible. Intuition to me feels less tangible. It's more a feeling or a hunch. But awareness is about being aware of who you are, who the people around you are, seeing and seizing opportunities, being very alert, and knowing when and how to act. I think being alert is key. It is about being practical and focused, even though at the time I didn't really know what I was focused on yet. I didn't know where the path was heading, I just knew I had to be on that path, if that makes sense. It's the same when writing a book. You know the beginning. But you don't know how it's going to end when you start writing it. I'm sure you had the same while you were writing this book.

What does surrendering mean to you?

To me, surrender is about feeling the energy that is here, right now. I know it sounds vague so I will explain what I mean with a few examples.

Quite frankly, when you first told me about the concept of surrender, I had a resistance to the word 'surrender' and tried to find a better way to say it. My first reaction to the word was that it meant giving up or seeing yourself as weak. However, the way you talk about surrendering is actually the opposite of giving up. It is accepting the current reality and what the truth is within that reality, versus resisting it. In the context of the awareness and intuition we spoke about earlier, it is about being alert to what is going on right now and tuning into the energy. Knowing that what comes up is true, because you feel the energy, even though you might have to admit it is the opposite of what you thought was right when you started.

To illustrate this with an example; when I first met my husband, he was still living in Europe, so it wasn't easy, especially when looking at it from the outside. But I completely surrendered to the flow of a beautiful and incredibly powerful energy that was streaming between and through us. And it has brought me more happiness than anything else ever has.

In the end, energy is the number one most important thing. New York taught me that. In that respect I did the same thing with New York when I came here for the first time. I literally surrendered to the city, and changed course depending on the energy I felt in New York and where it led me.

Chapter 4:
I Am You

"Survival is the second law of life. The first is that we are all one."

Joseph Campbell, writer and lecturer

On a subatomic level, matter is energy and every single one of us is part of the same energetic field.

In essence: the only way to be successful in personal and professional life, long-term, is to create win-win situations. This is quite contrary to Machiavellian philosophies and business practices.

I remember when I was doing my Masters degree in the late 1990s; it was the prime time of the alpha (fe)male. Being a good leader meant you were dominant, even a bit aggressive, although most people preferred to call it 'assertive'.

Good leaders were known to be competitive and give clear directions in a persuasive way. They were (or appeared to be) more intelligent, and people would follow their lead mostly because of their strong character.

The carrot and stick approach in leadership was commonly used to motivate people, with positive reinforcements as well as scaring them with punishments if their performance was not up to expectation. Unfortunately, in those days, fear-based leadership was more the norm than the exception.

Thankfully, that type of leadership style has become much less popular. People are slowly but surely realizing that it is far more effective to be a 'humble' leader.

Humble doesn't mean shy, or weak as some would argue, rather it means that someone is open both intellectually and emotionally to learn from those around them. Someone who keeps an open mind and heart. Someone who listens, has empathy, compassion, and is genuinely interested.

The textbook definition of empathy is the ability to understand and share the feelings of another. Empathy literally means you are able to empathize with someone else. Meaning, you are able to place yourself fully in that other person's position. And feel what they are feeling.

While empathy is the ability to feel what another person is feeling, compassion takes it one step further in realizing we all have similar sufferings, and you have a desire to truly diminish the suffering you see around you. One needs empathy to get to compassion.

Compassion is not feeling sorry for someone. Quite the contrary. It is a form of love. Now there's a big word.

Love.

To quote the Dalai Lama: "In simple terms, compassion and love can be defined as positive thoughts and feelings that give rise to such essential things in life as hope, courage, determination, and inner strength. In the Buddhist tradition, compassion and love are seen as two aspects of the same thing: compassion is the wish for another being to be free from suffering; love is wanting them to have happiness."

You could say that empathy is somewhat more passive and compassion is active, but don't mistake that as empathy not being relevant or not helping another person.

Just think about the times you were going through a tough period in your life; let's say a break-up. And your best friend came over and just sat next to you. The mere fact that you know your best friend is empathising with you alleviates your pain. The same applies to good things that happen in your life. Empathy doesn't just apply when people are struggling or in pain. Think back to when you graduated from college or got your first promotion. Didn't it feel better when people around you felt the joy together with you? Or when you celebrated it with loved ones?

Humans are social creatures and we are designed to feel part of a whole. It is my conviction that we actually are part of a bigger whole.

By practising empathy and compassion you come to realize that, deep down, we all have similar drivers, and at the basis of them all is either love or fear. I read the book "The Seat of the Soul", by Gary Zukav almost two decades ago, and it left a big impact on me, especially how he talks about love and fear and how they are at the basis of how we process emotions. I believe, all emotions can be seen as a derivative of either love or fear. Just think about that for a minute.

When you get jealous of, say, a colleague who seems to do everything right, isn't there fear at the core of that emotion? Aren't you merely afraid they might get promoted before you? The same logic applies to anger. When you get upset with your teenage daughter for staying out too late, aren't you actually just scared that something might happen to her?

And, likewise, on a more positive note, when you are basking with joy for having lost 20lbs of weight, doesn't that come down to self-love?

Just try this logic on all emotions that you might be feeling during the day, and you will find that at the core is either love and/or fear.

But let's go back to compassion. As I mentioned earlier, compassion makes you realize that we all have similar sufferings. This also creates the awareness that we are all connected. Once you realize we are somehow all connected, your whole attitude changes and, in return, people respond to you in a much more positive way.

It's hard to put a finger on it, and yet it's a very tangible feeling. Being in the presence of someone who has high levels of empathy and compassion is instantly recognizable. They radiate a sense of calm, peace, and authority at the same time. It draws people to them as well.

Once you practise empathy and compassion, you'll notice everything starts shifting. You become more patient, more friendly, and you get along with people much better. Even if people around you are not aware of what you are doing, they will definitely feel a difference. You become more magnetic.

No matter what type of work you do, I'm sure you can recall the difference between a manager or people you've worked with who have high levels of empathy versus low.

I was lucky to have been exposed to such a different leadership style during my first job at Unilever. I was working for the Knowledge Management Group, which was founded and led by Manfred Aben. He is the subject of this chapter's case study, in which you will find his personal thoughts on the topic of empathy and leadership.

What I noticed immediately about his leadership style was that Manfred truly listened to the people on his team. More importantly, he coached us to align with our own intentions, making sure that, as a team, we ended up with a common vision, rooted in everyone's individual intentions.

The key was that he really did listen to the people on his team. Listening is at the core of empathy. *Really* listening will enable you to put yourself in that person's place. Manfred's approach created a certain culture in our team, and it wasn't just him who listened. That was the beauty of it; everyone mirrored the behaviour that made the department not only a pleasant place to work, but also a very successful one.

The phenomenon of empathy or compassion being contagious is backed up by research. Social scientists James Fowler of UC San Diego and Nicolas Christakis of Harvard have demonstrated in their research that helping is contagious. It turns out that when managers are compassionate and kind, employees are more likely to want to behave in the same way. Cooperative and compassionate behaviour actually cascades in groups of people. Whenever someone was treated kindly, they wanted to extend that behaviour towards others as well.

And that's exactly the behaviour I observed in that department. We felt heard and appreciated. And we wanted to continue that type of behaviour within and outside our department, work together to achieve our goals, and help each other in the process. The vision was set by our leader, and supported by each of our individual objectives and underlying intentions. By means of Manfred coaching us and setting this precedence, people listened to each other, creating a strong support mechanism within the team and keeping everyone's eye on the same prize.

It actually reminded me of the story of Ubuntu, a South African folk tale that describes a beautiful philosophy.

Chapter 4: I Am You

A South African tale

An anthropologist had been studying the habits and customs of the Ubuntu tribe in Africa. When he finished his study he had to wait for transportation that would take him to the airport to return home. He was surrounded by the children of the tribe, so to help pass the time before he left, he proposed a game for the children to play.

He'd bought lots of candy and sweets in the city, so put everything in a basket with a beautiful ribbon attached. He placed the basket under a solitary tree and then he called the kids together. He drew a line on the ground and explained that they should wait behind the line for his signal. When he said "Go!" they should rush over to the basket. The first to arrive would win all the candies.

When he said "Go!" they all unexpectedly held each other's hands and ran towards the tree as a group. Once there, they simply shared the candy with each other and happily ate it.

The anthropologist was very surprised. He asked why they had gone together, especially if the first to arrive at the tree could have won everything in the basket – all the sweets.

A young girl simply replied: "How can one of us be happy if all the others are sad?"

The anthropologist was dumbfounded! For months he'd been studying the tribe, yet it was only now that he really understood their true essence…

"Africans have a thing called ubuntu. It is about the essence of being human; it is part of the gift that Africa will give the world. It embraces hospitality, caring about others and being willing to go the extra mile for the sake of another. We believe that a person is a person through other persons, that my humanity is caught up, bound up, inextricably, with yours. When I dehumanise you, I inexorably dehumanise myself. The solitary human being is a contradiction in terms. Therefore you seek to work for the common good because your humanity comes into its own in community, in belonging." ***Archbishop Desmond Tutu***

Case study: Leading with empathy

An interview with Manfred Aben, Vice President, Unilever R&D and China R&D Site Leader, Shanghai, China

I had the privilege of starting my career with a manager that instinctively led his team with empathy. He personally coached everyone in his department to make sure each one of us was reaching our fullest potential and contributed optimally to the business results. So when I was thinking about who to interview for the topic of empathy, I decided to reach out to Manfred Aben. I was delighted he accepted my invitation.

I met with Manfred via video conferencing. The last time I had seen him in person was when I was in Singapore two years prior to teach a graduate class. I had swung by the Unilever offices to say hello to old colleagues. And today, despite the fact it was 7am in Jakarta, Manfred was his usual energetic self, even on camera.

Manfred, can you please tell us a little bit about your background and how you ended up where you are now?

I've been with Unilever for more than 20 years, since 1995, and have spent most of it in R&D leadership roles. I started in knowledge management and have changed jobs every three years, because I like to take on new challenges. I've been in global, local, and regional roles across many categories. I have led multi-cultural teams across Europe, Asia, and Africa, and lived in the Netherlands, Singapore, and am currently in Indonesia.

Most of these roles have involved change: changing cultures and mindsets, ways of working, or organizational structures.

So what does leadership mean to you?

Leadership is about having a positive impact on people. Leadership is not about the title; it's about impact. It's about influencing people's behaviour or the results of their behaviour. It's about tapping into the talents and skills that people have, versus trying to mould them in a certain way.

Leadership is also about setting a clear vision, which doesn't have to be a static thing. A good leader makes people connect with their own vision. It's a journey.

In the end I think it's about awareness. It's not necessarily about inventing something new.

Key words that come to my mind when I think about leadership are: listening, inner purpose, openness, connectedness, and integrity.

One of the things I love to do is to coach people. As a coach, I am impartial to the results people want to achieve. What is their purpose? But as a manager I have an interest in what they want to achieve. So as a coaching manager, I take into consideration if and how their inner purpose can be aligned to the company's objectives.

Purpose is a heart-driven, emotional thing. And it's important to really have conversations with colleagues about this.

Interestingly, what you notice when you do this is that deep down, people really aren't all that different. Whether you are from Asia, Africa, or Europe, we all have common drivers. You discover that once you go deeper. You just need to go to the level of underlying intentions. When you link your objectives to your intentions, you pass a few rational stages before entering the emotional stages. For example, you go from wanting to make a profit, to wanting to be loved. And when you are coaching someone you instantly notice the shift when they are really getting down to that level. The shift from the rational to the emotional. When that shift happens, options open up versus closing down.

Can you please explain what you mean by that?

Well, fundamentally we are all human beings and we want to be part of a human community. It boils down to wanting to fulfil deeper desires like love, respect, a sense of belonging, and a deeper meaning to life.

Trying to understand why people want to achieve what they want to achieve, is by far the most important thing for a leader to do. The critical bit is to get people to connect with their own intentions and purpose. Because once they do that, you can find a common ground. And that common ground can ensure it all ties back to the company's purpose. I think the key word here is 'authenticity'. When you are true and authentic, you connect to your intentions. And when you connect to your intentions, you have a completely different drive and motivation to do your job.

What does empathy mean to you?

Empathy is 'feeling with'. It comes from the Greek word *pathos*, meaning feeling sympathy, 'suffering with' even, but I personally don't think it's that feeling of suffering. I think empathy means you are able to put yourself in the shoes of somebody else.

In my opinion, empathy is awareness. You cannot have empathy without having awareness. Having awareness of yourself, awareness of your surroundings and the people around you, awareness of the eternal dialogue that goes on inside your head.

Another element of empathy is love. You cannot be empathetic if you don't love people. It's not about sharing the same perspective. It is about *understanding* the different perspectives and not forcing these perspectives to converge.

Empathy is also about being aware of your assumptions, and the willingness to let these go. It is about really listening to the person in front of you. Everyone listens with filters. The key is to be aware of your own filters and biases.

Having empathy means you have a real understanding for other people's circumstances. Coaching and leadership is an important tool for this. It's important to understand where the other parties are coming from, versus making all kinds of assumptions. Empathy is about testing other people's assumptions, as well as your own.

The basis of empathy is that the root values are shared with most people. But, likewise, it is also about understanding and accepting the differences.

As I mentioned before, authenticity is key.

How do you see the link between empathy and achieving business results?

I think that's a no brainer. Results in the end come down to individual people. If individuals are not working optimally, you will make losses.

Without awareness and empathy you can only tell people what to do. But with empathy you can make sure their vision aligns with the company's purpose. It is a direct efficiency equation. Happier people perform better. And not only that; it's the right thing to do. Making sure people are happy. And the best way to do that is by tapping into their inner drivers and motivations.

When our current CEO, Paul Polman, came on board, he created a vision that was focused on sustainable living. The idea was to double growth, while halving the impact on the environment, but doubling the social impact. It has made our company incredibly attractive to work for because people love to work in a company with a purpose.

And the results are incredible and self-evident.

Chapter 5:
Vulnerability

"You can't get to courage without walking through vulnerability."

Brené Brown, scholar, author, and public speaker

As a mother of a young baby, I only recently really learned the true meaning of vulnerability. When you have to hand over your little one into the hands of a stranger because you have to work, you feel more vulnerable than you could ever have imagined before.

The only other two times that I felt truly vulnerable were when I quit my secure and well-paid consulting job to start my own company, and when I told my (now) husband that I loved him, before he had told me.

We had only been dating for a few months, and were dancing vivaciously on the dance floor at the Annual Sailors Ball in New York City. I felt it so strongly with my whole heart, I just blurted out: "I love you!"

The response? Silence. Plus two very big eyes staring at me with a unique blend of horror and shock.

And you might think that I would feel shame or fear at that moment, but nothing could be further from the truth. I felt an enormous amount of power and courage. The shame and fear did come slightly the next day, when I realized what I had done, but even then, I still was proud and happy I had opened up to him. From that day onwards I noticed he was also becoming more fully engaged in our relationship.

One year later, we were married and expecting a baby.

I'm not saying that every story where you dare to be vulnerable has a happy ending like this. But I do believe it requires vulnerability to get to a place of courage. And vice versa, it takes courage to be vulnerable.

It is important to stop focusing on feelings like fear or shame rooted in worrying about what other people think of you. In the end, people will think what they want to think. It's actually none of our business what they think. It's theirs. And it's certainly not in our control.

Vulnerability is also about embracing our darkness. As Einstein allegedly once said: "Darkness is in reality the absence of light." Whether or not Einstein was the one who said it, this statement rings true to me. But you won't be able to bring the darkness to light if you don't acknowledge or have awareness of it first. People have elements of light and darkness within them, and that's OK. It is when you are ignorant, ignore, deny, or give in to your less desirable traits and thoughts, that they become more powerful.

The key point is that in essence, there is no such thing as darkness. It's merely the absence of light. So the dark is really only dark when we don't cast a light over something. This all sounds very abstract, I know, so let's look at this with a real-life example.

Let's take a 'dark' emotion like jealousy. If a direct co-worker of yours is getting promoted to a position you were hoping for, that can cause feelings of jealousy, which of course is very human. Now, when you don't consciously observe and acknowledge the fact you are jealous, it will translate into certain behaviours in the office and towards your co-worker or people in your team – or perhaps even the people you love at home. But if you were to stand still and fully observe what is going on inside of you, and accept those feelings for what they are without resistance, you will notice that the strong feelings slowly subside.

So bringing to light means bringing your full attention to what is going on inside. Your observations will lead to insights and awareness. And the moment you reach awareness around a certain negative emotion, it will slowly lose its power over you.

Just as with the concept of surrender, being vulnerable also has this element of letting go of control.

Being vulnerable brings with it a lot of uncertainty. You don't know for sure how people or circumstances will respond and, yes, you stand the chance of getting hurt, because you are emotionally open.

So, then, why would we want to take that chance?

If you have read the books of Brené Brown or have seen her famous TED Talk, then you have heard about her ground breaking research in the areas of shame and vulnerability. She talks about 'wholehearted' people.

According to Brown in her book *Daring Greatly*, "The wholehearted are people that don't shy away from being vulnerable, and they live their lives from a place of worthiness. This gives them courage and compassion which leads to true connections. They embrace their vulnerabilities and the fact that they (and everyone else) are imperfect. But no matter what happens, they know they are worthy of love and belonging."

According to her research, vulnerability is the birthplace of joy, love, and creativity.

But why are most of us so guarded against vulnerability? I think the answer to that question can often be traced back to childhood. When I look at my own life, it's fair to say I literally had to unlearn always holding up a brave face, or being 'perfect' in many ways – first of all when it came to work and study.

I grew up in the most loving home imaginable. Being the youngest of four, and having the sweetest parents and siblings imaginable in the world, I can honestly say I would not trade my family for anyone else's in the world. They have been instrumental in making me successful in both my personal and professional life. Their unconditional love has made me a self-confident, loving individual. I have always had lots of friends and I have been pretty successful in almost every challenge I've been up against.

My parents have also always been my best advisers and supporters throughout my life. They were instrumental in making me long for perfection, which can be both an asset as well as a possible hindrance to success. I remember when I was a young girl, I would come home with 98 points for a maths test, and my father would say: "That's great! But what happened to the two points?" A minor event like that can leave quite a big impact on a young person. I took what he said very literally and thought I had to be perfect all the time. However, only later in life, I realized that what he meant was: always do the best that you can, which is the best advice you can ever give anyone.

Perfectionism has a lot of advantages. But it can become paralysing when you let your fears and insecurities rule over your dreams and passions. When you are more concerned about what others will think of you when they realize you are not perfect.

For example, I have longed to be a writer for as long as I can remember. As a little child I was always writing short stories, and my mother would tell me that she could see me becoming a writer one day. She planted a seed in my head when I was seven or eight years old, and I have held on to that dream for as long as I can remember. And yet I went on to study economics, and a Masters in business and marketing, while deep down my dream was to be an author.

Why did it take me so long to pursue my heart's desire?

Writing involves vulnerability. There is something extremely scary about sharing deep, personal thoughts and feelings on paper with others. It feels like you are exposing your soul to the world. But fear is an interesting emotion. Because once you confront your fears, they seem to fade away.

Perhaps the best way to describe this is through a traditional story in philosophy that talks about this very topic.

The Shadow
author unknown

"In a remote mountain village, the head of the village died and leadership was passed on to his son.

Throughout time, the people of the village had lived for many years under the control of a huge monster that loomed like a shadow over the village.

Whenever anyone tried to find freedom, this large shadow appeared with a loud voice echoing through the mountains. The villagers always retreated at the sight of the dark image.

The young man who was now the leader realized the time had come to confront this monster. He went out with a group of villagers, and as soon as they appeared at the edge of the village the huge shadow appeared. They stepped back in fright.

The young man observed how the shadow became bigger and the voice louder as they retreated. He paused and then bravely took a step towards the shadow. It seemed to become slightly smaller. He stepped again and his view was confirmed, the shadow became less and the voice less powerful.

He continued moving towards it until at his feet was the source of the shadow. He plucked up this small ephemeral object in his hand and asked: ***"Who are you?"***

"Fear" was the weak, feeble reply.

The young man closed his hand and the fear disappeared entirely."

Clearly the moral of this story is about facing our fears. When we actually dare to look at our fears by observing and accepting them, they are much more likely to pass through us rather than own us.

Case study: Living from authenticity

An interview with Jennifer Barckley, founder of Makers & Tastemakers

In this case study I have the honour to collect the thoughts of Jennifer Barckley. Jennifer is a former client turned friend. From the moment I met Jennifer, I knew she was an extraordinary human being. Not only is she an absolute inspiration to work with, but she is so real and so true to herself that I knew she would be the perfect leader to talk to for the topic of vulnerability.

While most of my interviews were over the phone or in person, Jennifer and I were mostly in correspondence via email. With the time difference between Colorado (where I had moved to in the meantime) and Amsterdam, I asked Jennifer if she would prefer a phone call or me sending her the questions so she could think about her responses and email me her thoughts. She opted for email, and in typical Jennifer style, she took so much time and effort to answer all questions in so much detail and flair, that I cannot take any credit for the case study below. It was all written and thought of by Jennifer herself.

Jennifer, can you please tell us a little bit about your background and how you ended up where you are now?

Working hard, really hard, is somehow baked into my DNA. Maybe it's because I was born one month premature, weighing less than three pounds, to a strong-willed mother hooked up to a dialysis machine to keep her kidneys kicking. Maybe it's because my dad is a smart engineer with a tremendous work ethic who made my school lunch every morning before starting his own day, all with nonchalant humility. The reason doesn't really matter. Yet, it led me from the soulful city of Portland, Oregon, to New York City at the age of 18.

From the moment I stepped off the plane, I didn't stop moving, starting with an internship at a prestigious couture fashion house, coupled with multiple jobs, crew team practice at 6am, partying (it was college after all) and a close-to-perfect grade point average. Nearing graduation four years later, at the age of 21, I landed my dream job as the PR manager for a natural and organic skin-care company. After seven years of leading brand-marketing communications – building campaigns, websites, a magazine, a flagship store and a spa, launching a training programme, working in Germany and more – it was time to move on. I dabbled in entrepreneurship with my own 'pro-social' (do good with good clients) consulting firm, before going on to lead brand-marketing communications for a large, socially-minded global beauty company.

After 12 aggregate career years, something – let's call it meditative perspective – shifted. Having worked with the aforementioned large, global, and 'natural' beauty company for the past few years, religiously tracking daily sales, I realized that this – a job intrinsically intertwined with the corporate rat race – was not the sustainable life I envisioned.

Sure, my life was seemingly perfect, privileged, in fact. I lived in Manhattan's Upper West Side with access to organic dry cleaning, over-priced green juices, the most bustling Whole Foods in the world, Central Park, premium barre workouts, luxury fashion, ballets and ballads, and regular business travel. And while truly grateful for all the enriching opportunities and access I had, I felt stuck and out of alignment with my inner vision.

I yearned to call forth on my courage and be entrepreneurial – letting go of fear, of attachment to my beloved wardrobe, a small yet covetable NYC apartment, job status, and a healthy salary to boot. And there was no running away from the voice whispering and slowly shouting within. I needed to give myself permission to live, to really live. To start embracing my dreams, including the vision to seriously live abroad, most notably in Amsterdam, the Netherlands.

So, sparing some undramatic details, I took the mental leap, found a client across the pond, built a business plan for my new brand consultancy, cleaned my closets, and asked my forever-compassionate husband to join me on this journey. That was in November 2015.

Four months later, the sun is setting over Amsterdam, and I can't keep my eyes off a peaceful bird perched on a branch overhanging my neighbour's quiet terrace. Watching a fluttering friend simply sit, mundane as it may sound, is thrilling. From the frenetic pace of New York City – a place I still call home in my heart – to the quaint cobblestoned streets of Amsterdam, I'm finding my way back to the basics. To me.

Can you talk a bit about your current role, scope, and responsibilities?

I am the founder of Makers & Tastemakers, a consultancy company focused on branding, marketing, communications, and leadership development. I am committed to helping people and brands build and grow into innovative leaders, through authenticity, clear goals, sound strategies, and smart tactics. My mission with this consultancy is to authentically develop people and brands into courageous, different-driving leaders.

Through that lens, I am currently working on two key projects. One is to build and solidify the brand identity (purpose-led mission, etc) for a leading global trend firm. The other is to build a new digital social venture. As the CMO, I am working closely with the founder to build the brand ID, create and launch the marketing strategy, refine the brand's website and app that's in development, and much more – wearing many hats, as tends to be the case in a lean start-up team.

What does leadership mean to you?

Leadership, to me, is guiding, rallying, supporting, and cultivating people on their path to greatness. It's a partnered journey in discovery – helping others to unlock their own potential through Socratic questioning, brainstorming, 360-degree feedback and, from a business perspective, shared commitment to results. By doing that, I've learned it takes a lot of courage, vulnerability, and empathy to truly lead others.

In order to earn trust among your team and to actually begin leading, you first need to show up as your authentic self.

How would you define awareness and how does it link to leadership?

Awareness is another way of saying 'consciousness'. It's listening to your intuitive inner voice. And it's listening to others, not just with your ears but also with your heart.

Leadership is a dance, a partnership. Nudging others to move with you towards a common goal while giving them the space to guide and lead, on a shared path to greatness, and making the difference you seek to create. In order to do this dance, you need to be aware of where you're going and how your steps effect and affect others. And you need to pause and listen to others, in order to understand where they want to go and where they are going. Are they still dancing with you?

What does vulnerability mean to you, and how do you incorporate it in your personal life and at work?

Vulnerability is living from authenticity – even when it's hard and it hurts, and you want to run away, far and fast. To me, vulnerability is intrinsically linked to courage and being courageous. In her infamous Ted Talk on vulnerability, my virtual vulnerability guru Brené Brown said that courage, as a word, is built from the Latin word cur, meaning: "To tell the story of who you are with your whole heart." This, to me, is real vulnerability.

For the past year, I've had a somewhat obsessive focus on being vulnerable and living vulnerably. As a perfectionist, I have to make a really conscious choice to be imperfect, to be vulnerable, moment-by-moment. So I constantly and consciously choose to push myself beyond the protective sheath I'd prefer to put around myself; instead, exposing and sharing what I really think, feel, need, and want from myself and from others.

For instance, I recently shared with my husband that I wasn't feeling happy and I needed to choose a different path – hence our shared decision to move to

Amsterdam, just a few months ago. Being vulnerable is now less of a fight (within myself) and even less of a conscious effort. It's simply becoming a way of being and of living – in full embrace.

At work I show up as myself. I share what's going on in my personal life because I believe that people work with and for people – real humans. In my experience the added benefit is that the more open I am, the more others are inclined to be open and honest, too. And I push myself every day to share where I'm challenged, stuck, or concerned. Working as a start-up and with start-ups, I think it's especially important to be open with my team members about my own pitfalls – like my desire to get something perfect before I launch. And to openly, vulnerably, ask others for feedback to reveal blind spots that I just don't know exist, so we can align and grow as a team.

What has been the effect on the people you work with (and yourself)?

In projecting a bit, I think people often feel inspired, empowered, committed, and valued. My current focus is to give people the space to lead, which also means me letting go a bit. I'm amazed at what people can ideate and create when you open a window and say in some constellation of words, "I trust you. Go for it. I'm here to support you along the way." To be clear, this is very much a work in progress for me. I've seen that it can truly work to create an open, honest, and inspired work environment.

Chapter 6:
Insanity

"The distance between insanity and genius is measured only by success."

Bruce Feirstein, screenwriter, and humorist

Have you ever wondered what the definition of normal is? It literally means: according to the norms. Also known as: conforming to a standard, to the usual, typical, or expected. As we grow up, society teaches us that when we are acting in a way that counters prevailing norms of conduct, we are being rebellious or even crazy. But if everybody were to remain 'normal' or stick to the rules, then nothing would ever change.

I remember saying to one of my best friends a few years ago: "Who in their right mind would ever want to be normal?" And I still stand by that statement.

When we look at the world today, I think it's fair to say that things are not always the way they are supposed to be. And yet, they are today's norms. So when I talk about insanity in the context of this book, I am referring to a state of mind or behaviour that is outside of the prevailing norms.

I am convinced that a little hint (or actually a good chunk) of 'craziness' is required in order to be a good leader, and especially to inspire those around you.

Again, I am not talking about mental disorders. They are not to be downplayed in terms of their seriousness, nor wished upon anyone.

But it is my conviction that being different from what appears to be normal can actually be a very good thing.

You see, when you are normal, you are not challenging the status quo. And you are definitely not vibrating an energy that people want to follow.

I once read a brilliant quote on one of those little magnets on my best friend's fridge: "If you know someone normal, then you probably don't know them very well." At first I thought it was just funny, but then I realized it was probably one of the most profound sentences I had read in a while.

One of my all-time favourite authors, Paulo Coelho, once wrote: "Stay mad, but behave like normal people. Run the risk of being different, but learn to do so without attracting attention." Interesting statement for sure.

Should we all stay guarded and attempt to hide behind our masks, just so we can fit in society the way it is expected? Or should we aim for a different type of society, one where people are accepted for who they really are, even if they appear to be 'abnormal' and everyone evolves more quickly because we push each other's boundaries and norms?

Interestingly, Paulo Coelho also said: "I want to continue being crazy; living my life the way I dream it, and not the way the other people want it to be. I succeeded because I was crazy enough to think I could."

Isn't it a leader's primary role to push people in a positive way? To make sure they reach their fullest potential? Isn't creativity the ultimate form of stepping outside of the norms? How else would you be able to do something that is novel and interesting to the world?

An animated video by agency Leo Burnett Detroit tells the full story (Source: Leo Burnett Detroit, "Book Burning Party – Troy Library", January 20, 2012. <https://vimeo.com/35758683>). The local library was known to be beautiful, busy, and award winning. Sadly, when the economic recession hit in 2011, times were hard for Troy and the city no longer had enough money for its library. What followed was a planned vote, where the inhabitants were asked if they would agree to a small tax increase to preserve the library. This angered an anti-tax group, which was well organized and well funded. It started dominating the conversation and the topic's focus went from preserving the beautiful library, to increased taxes.

Meanwhile, an organization called Safeguarding American Families came out and started putting signs up that said: "Book-burning party August 5". Obviously the whole idea of burning books was bad enough, but turning it proudly into a party aggravated a lot of people. What followed was a social media sensation. People started posting comments on the Facebook page the group had created, sharing posts and tweeting about the upcoming event being outrageous. How could people celebrate the burning of books? But Safeguarding American Families did not stop there. It created videos, portraying more disturbing content around burning books, and having fun while doing so. It tweeted obscene quotes like: "The Troy library might be short on money, but it has books to burn." It even had items for sale, like book bags emblazoned with the words "book-burning party". It posted newspaper ads and flyers for book-burning party babysitters, and even lined up entertainment to perform during the book-burning party.

People responded en mass, shocked, and started posting and commenting on social media: "You guys are booking a band?" People were enraged. Some quotes on social media: "Why would you burn books, idiots!" "Cheap imbeciles!" "What has this world come to?"

These people posted their own links, shared with friends, debated the merits of libraries and the audacity of burning books. The conversation started snowballing and spread from Facebook to city council meetings, from newspapers to TV! It grew from national to international news.

Once the whole discussion reached its peak, the so-called Safeguarding American Families revealed the true intent of its campaign: "A vote against the library is like a vote to burn books." And it turned out that the organization itself was a hoax, invented by the advertising agency Leo Burnett, which wanted to stop the discussion from focusing on taxes and instead realize how horrible it is to close a library like the Troy's. People started posting, tweeting, and reporting all over again, but this time they were in favour of the library. The conversation had changed completely. It went back from taxes to the actual topic in hand, which was the library.

When it was time to vote, there was a huge turnout from people in favour of saving the library. And the library won.

Clearly, this is an example where taking a big risk and acting in a way that's outrageous has an amazing impact on the people, and is quite inspiring.

Another example would be from Richard Branson, one of my favourite businessmen. In my opinion he is the embodiment of daring to be different. He describes himself as, "A tie-loathing adventurer and thrill-seeker who believes in turning ideas into reality. Otherwise known as Dr Yes at Virgin!"

One of Branson's most memorable events would probably be when he dressed up as Spider-Man in London, and hung down from a skyscraper to raise money for a local hospital. Or starting a business to venture out into space! Then there were a number of businesses that did not succeed, including Virgin Cola and Virgin Brides. But you don't hear Branson being sorry about these endeavours. Quite the contrary. One of his key traits is that he sees what other people call 'failures' as an opportunity to learn. To quote Richard Branson himself:

"My mother drummed into me from an early age that I should not spend much time regretting the past. I try to bring that discipline to my business career. Over the years, my team and I have not let mistakes, failures, or mishaps get us down. Instead, even when a venture has failed, we try to look for opportunities, to see whether we can capitalize on another gap in the market."

Another key characteristic that an inspiring leader should have is a sense of idealism or even naivety.

To be 'insane' enough to believe in an idea, you also need to be a little naïve, or a word I like more is 'idealist'. Unfortunately, people usually don't see this as a positive thing, but I would have to disagree with mainstream thought. Having and keeping an open mind, just like a child, actually keeps us curious and believing in things that other people might believe to be impossible. So in that sense, being naïve or idealistic can actually be a very good thing.

In life coaching, one of the key things at the foundation of any breakthrough in life is acknowledging one's limiting beliefs. What do I mean by this?

Basically, we shape our lives based on the beliefs that we hold and this ties back to the stories we tell ourselves, as I described in chapter one.

Imagine a frog sitting at the bottom of a well. What would it see if it were to look up? To the frog, the small surface of sky seems to be the whole sky, but if the frog came to the surface of the well, it would discover a much bigger sky.

Chapter 6: Insanity

This metaphor merely shows the importance of perspective and being aware of your own perspective as well as others around you, especially as a leader.

Like individuals, societies hold certain (limiting) beliefs as well. I'm sure the group of frogs in the well could declare the frog that believes in the full sky as insane. This is what often happens in society as well. The first person wanting to fly to the moon was most likely seen as crazy.

Once we realize how many of our own thoughts, as well as our society's thoughts, are limiting, only then will we be able to break free from them. But often, these limiting beliefs are blind spots. It takes a lot of awareness, most importantly self-awareness, to first identify limiting beliefs and then to change them.

Case study: Insanity

An interview with Anita Keij, finance and sustainability expert

Insanity is probably one of my favourite concepts in this book, as it is the wild-card and the one with the most passion.

I immediately hoped that Anita Keij, one of my dearest friends from college, would be willing to share her thoughts on the topic. She has always been such an inspiration to me, predominantly because she has always been someone to follow her dreams and passions. Her passion has led her on the most amazing adventures and ventures, and enabled her to be extremely successful and accomplished.

Anita and I have had several video conferences and phone calls, as well as email correspondence, to gather her thoughts on the topic of insanity. Being the double Masters economics and philosophy graduate that Anita is, it was easy to get lost in our discussions – in a good way. And without realizing it, we would spend hours on the phone. After a few weeks of going back and forth over email, I gathered many of Anita's valuable insights and interesting thoughts on this concept of insanity.

Anita, can you please tell us a little bit about your background and how you ended up where you are today?

I work primarily in the field of finance and sustainability. My professional interests are investing, sustainable development, and business ethics. How I reached where I am now has been an exciting and unorthodox journey. After studying economics and philosophy, I worked for many years in commercial and development banking. I worked in the western world as well as in emerging markets for companies like Rabobank and FMO, the Dutch development bank. I also worked for NGOs and a social enterprise in frontier markets. I lived in the Democratic Republic of the Congo, where I was first in the Frankfurt Zoological Society team and then CEO consultant at Virunga Social Enterprise. There, it was all about sustainable business – and the socio-economic development of the region to support conservation of the magnificent Virunga National Park. This park is very special because it is home to the last mountain gorillas. I have also worked for *National Geographic*, a magazine I've admired ever since I was a little girl. So, as you can see, I've contributed to very diverse companies and institutions across the globe, but the common thread has always been my passions and interests. All of those experiences combined brought me to where I am now, in this specific field of interest. I'm currently still working with FMO, as well as with Virunga National Park as a sideline, and I'm lecturing at the University of Innsbruck on the topic of business ethics. In my spare time I'm a ski instructor as well, believe it or not.

What are your personal interests?

First of all, for me, personal life and work completely blend together, and I wouldn't want it any other way. It's very important that I feel connected to what I do for a living. My passions are nature, wildlife, and outdoor sports, and you can see all of those reflected in the work that I do.

What does leadership mean to you?

Leadership to me means bringing individuals together, it means cooperation in the first place, but also coordination. It means creating mutual understanding and acceptance. Leadership is human nature, and in principle I believe that humans are animals. Our behaviour has certain patterns, dynamics. Being or following a leader is part of our lifestyle (or, basically it is a survival technique), and we can learn a lot from the animal kingdom. They actually do a lot better than human beings in many regards.

How would you define a good leader?

Being a good leader should be something natural. A good leader is charismatic and inspiring. Authenticity and integrity is key. Good leaders are passionate about what they are doing. They believe in something, and are able to make others believe in it, too. A vision is necessary, as well as flexibility. It's important to find the right balance there. Dare to stand for something, but also be open to progressive insights. It is about leading a group of individuals in such a way that it brings out the best of everyone. Ideally, people should feel happy and comfortable to give input, have a certain pride to contribute and are aligned with the goals. It's not a sum of the parts, but a synergy. A good leader creates willingness to realize something bigger together.

How would you define awareness?

Awareness is not only being aware of what you are aware of, but also, and especially, being aware of the greatness of the unknown. Respect this greatness, accept uncertainty, see the wonders around us, and expect the unexpected.

Awareness is about not taking things for granted, but actually being grateful for the things we have. It is about appreciating the laws of nature, its force and wholeness.

Awareness is also being true to your own nature and being critical where necessary. To me, it is about questioning human constructs, and finding your own values and morals (in a constructive way).

When leading, awareness is key. Be clear, be authentic, and avoid hypocrisy. Be aware of the fact that you know little; focus on the essentials, on key values. Trust. Be kind of naïve. Be playful. Many things are like a game. Sometimes even a gamble. Know what is at stake, try to be the best, but don't take anything or anybody (including yourself) too seriously.

What does insanity (or being different from the norm) mean to you?

Good question, and my relating question would be about the norm. What is the norm and why? And why is it perceived to be insane to not comply to (often) "arbitrary" norms? Is it because of the majority? The majority, however, doesn't make anything true, right, or good!

The majority of people take many things as being the truth, just like that. Or worse, certain behaviours can simply be inconsiderate or even hypocritical.

Structures. Rules. Traditions. As such, nothing wrong with these, as we need some common (undisputed) grounds to function, but we need to question things as kids do: "Why, why, why?" Try to say and do what you really want. Create personal freedom, of course with all the respect and responsibility required.

Is it insane to ask, to question, to create free space, to be curious, to wonder about things? I don't think so, as the world is full of miracles. Keep your eyes and senses wide open. Absorb, appreciate, play. Value what is. Enjoy diversity and surprises.

Act with passion, commitment, and dedication. Be crazy about things and people you love. 'Being insane' can motivate like crazy and can lead to insane, incredible achievements.

Don't be afraid to be different than the norm. Use new insights. Adjust. That's the way to progress. A key law of nature! As Darwin said, the most adaptive species survive. Changing or adapting sometimes means disobedience. In order to move forward, creativity is needed. Be a rebel sometimes.

Allowing yourself to be kind of insane is very liberating, too. It means being free, open, and non-judgmental.

When you don't worry about conforming to the expectations of others, it means being able to be authentic. It allows you to follow your dreams. Learn from others. And appreciate the (non-conforming) dreams and choices of others. It makes you confident and unpretentious at the same time. It makes life more fun!

How do you incorporate it into your work?

I actually don't like to see personal life and work as two different things. I find the term 'work-life-balance' absurd. As if work is not a part of life. As if most people do not spend more awake time with colleagues than with their partners, friends, and families.

But to give you a concrete example: when I decided to go to the Congo to work with mountain gorillas, after working for a bank and living in London for many years, people literally told me I was crazy. But I think that what they label as 'craziness' actually holds a lot of power and conviction. None of it was an easy process, but I feel lucky I had the courage to do it. I've been fascinated by the people, the nature, and the wildlife of that country. Believing you can contribute to a better world gives strength. In many ways, the Congo is both heaven and hell on Earth. And I like being part of a team that wants to improve circumstances in the country. You could call it a naïve belief, or an ideal. And even though most people don't like to be called naïve, I think it is something beautiful and pure.

Do you have any other thoughts on this topic?

To summarize, insanity is literally being crazy about something, which I think brings intrinsic motivation and focused energy. Truly believe and enjoy something, be dedicated to contribute to the process and the goal. For business and pleasure alike.

Chapter 7:
Joy

"When you do things from your soul, you feel a river moving in you, a joy."

Rumi, 13th-century Persian poet

Happiness is defined as a state of wellbeing and contentment, while joy is a feeling of great pleasure and happiness.

In the end, isn't a state of happiness and joy what we as human beings strive for? It is that ultimate state of being that many philosophers have analysed and written about in order to understand what it really means and how we can get there.

Sadly, research has shown that in the US, less than 50% of employees are happy at work (source: The Conference Board Job Satisfaction Survey, 2014), let alone joyful. This is a scary statistic given the time we all spend at work. It is shocking to realize that so many people are in jobs and careers that don't make them happy.

Being unhappy at work doesn't only affect individual employees. Apparently, companies with happy employees outperform their competition by 20%. And happy employees turn out to be 12% more productive.

This might explain why Google actually has a chief happiness officer, not that I am a big advocate of that either as it could potentially turn happiness into an asset worth chasing after to improve the bottom line. And it is a known fact that those who chase happiness are actually the least happy.

It begs the question: why are so many people unhappy at work? One explanation could be that a lot of people are making fear-driven decisions, and are drawn to careers they think will bring in a better pay cheque, more job security, or give them a higher level of prestige. I hear it in almost every semester I teach when I ask my students what they are majoring in and why. Often, students that choose, say, accounting give the rationale that they think it will secure them a job after graduation. But when I ask them what they like about the idea of being an accountant, other than the (potential) job security, their answers are often less than convincing.

However, it's not only about making the wrong career choice from the get-go.

Happiness is a choice, but that doesn't mean we have to spend our days chasing it. Joy cannot be a goal in that way. Joy is to be found in the journey, not in the result. So chasing after it, as if it's a pot of gold, is a doomed endeavour.

Then what are we supposed to do? Don't we all want to be happy and make sure that the people around us, including the ones we lead, are happy? Most definitely, and here are a few things we can do to increase our chances of finding joy at work, day to day, as well as to inspire others to find joy as well.

1. Choose a job, career, or occupation that fits you

As simple and logical as it sounds, in practice it really doesn't seem to be that simple at all. My husband always says "common sense isn't that common", and that applies to this point for sure. How often do you see a receptionist at a hospital who is just plain rude or unfriendly to a patient? Or an investment banker who, at heart, would rather work for a non-profit? The point is that it's important to pick something you love doing. Life is too short to do something you dislike, plus it affects the people around you in both directions, depending on whether you made the right choice or not.

Simply put, choose something that:
a) makes you smile when you think about it;
b) fits your personality;
c) helps you achieve your personal vision.

In other words, choose something that fits **who you really are.**

What you are doing has to feel *worthwhile* to you. For one person, doing something for a non-profit that betters the world feels worthwhile; while another may feel successful building a tech start-up that creates job opportunities for others.

Doing something meaningful does not mean you have to think about saving the world. Again, it comes down to having the self-awareness to know what is meaningful to you specifically.

2. Do not expect it to be easy

One of the biggest challenges I see with the current prevailing mindset is a certain sense of entitlement. In the western world we currently live in an instant-gratification era, where we can switch on the TV and choose from hundreds of channels and on-demand programmes, too. We may crave a pizza, order it, and it's at our doorstep within 20 minutes (or we get upset when it takes a full half hour to get to us, which is a pretty outrageous reaction when you think of it!).

Likewise, someone who graduated from Harvard might feel they are entitled to a certain type of job.

I remember on one occasion when we hired an intern. The intern was very smart and came from an excellent school, but she felt so entitled that she was not willing to work hard for anything, or do any of the 'dirty' jobs like coordinating logistics for a workshop.

This intern thought that by only doing what she wanted to do herself would bring her joy – which, in her case, was the more strategic tasks. But it really doesn't work that way. Having joy, and being able to spread the joy (as it is quite contagious) is not something that just gets handed to you like that, nor thrown in your lap. It is something that you yourself have to take full responsibility for, and work hard for. Anything worthwhile is worth working hard for. It actually becomes worthwhile when you work for it. Any experience in life that is worthwhile is at the same time also humbling to us as human beings. Because it teaches us something profound and makes us move beyond our ego. Bianca didn't last long in our company. She quit, as she wasn't happy, and it turned out that she remained that way for years to come. She kept changing jobs, as none of them gave her the joy she felt entitled to.

Another great example of joy not getting thrown in your lap is something I experienced myself while I was writing this book. Even though writing is what brings me great joy, the process of actually writing a book can be pretty painful. You have periods where you struggle to put three sentences on a page, and have insecurities about whether or not you are on the right track – the list goes on. But anything worthwhile requires effort, and being able to do it and achieving the task will bring great joy. But it cannot be joyful the whole time. Joy comes in bits and pieces, and in specific moments; when you have that ah-ha moment while working on a project, for example. Or when you see that you were able to really help that colleague or employee you've been coaching.

3. Lighten up

They key point here is to not take things too seriously. Playfulness is at the core of joy. A Zen monk once said: "If you're not laughing, then you're not getting it." True story. Innovation and creativity can only take place when you dare to play, laugh, and have fun in the process. Many things in life can be viewed as a game. That doesn't mean you don't respect it or don't give it your 100%, but looking at things like it is a game gives you a freshness and clarity in how you perceive a situation, versus being stressed out or too attached to the outcome of your efforts.

This brings me to the second point: being too attached to the outcome of your efforts. Earlier in this book I spoke about letting go of control, and surrendering as a key practice to gaining deeper levels of awareness and becoming a better leader. What is a direct consequence of that way of thinking is that you cannot be too attached to the outcome. You need faith and flexibility to be able to do that.

Faith, because you need to trust that after giving something 100%, you have to let go and know that whatever is meant to happen, will happen. I purposefully say 'after' giving something your full attention and 100%, because trusting the outcome and detaching yourself from the outcome does not mean not doing your very best to get the outcome you envisage. But putting your ego aside and realizing you might not know everything, including which outcome is the best for everyone involved, gives you enormous power and sense of freedom, and, ironically, the best outcome possible.

When you look at your business objectives as a game, you start becoming a better player and it all becomes more fun.

Having fun is extremely important, because it makes you spread a certain kind of energy that is very attractive to people – as well as contagious. Having a sense of humour in the office can do wonders for the morale of everyone there.

Smile at people. Show genuine interest and make a joke whenever it's appropriate. This makes people more relaxed and helps them to perform better.

4. Gratitude

Lastly, and most importantly, to get to a place of joy, you must show gratitude and be grateful. I will be focusing on gratitude fully in the next and final chapter, as it is the basis for happiness in general.

In a nutshell, the key is to consciously choose to look at the good that is around you, right now, in the present moment, and be grateful for them.

It is very easy to only focus on what is not going well.

But happiness is something we can experience when we choose to look at all the good things we have in each day, in each person, in every situation and circumstance.

We experience joy when we are truly living in the moment versus always chasing after something in the future or reminiscing the past. Observe the wonders that are around you in every moment, whether it is the beautiful bird singing outside, or your child's smile. These types of observations and moments of gratitude will bring you to a place of joy. The key is getting to that place of joy and living your life from that place. Once this is regularly practised, more joy comes into your life and it becomes a positive cycle.

And, in turn, making decisions and performing everyday tasks from a place of joy will not only lead to more fun, but also to better performance and results for yourself and the people you lead.

Getting in the flow

Joy will get you in the right flow – where inspiration takes its own course. This, however, requires practice.

Psychologist Mihaly Csikszentmihalyi's renowned investigations have revealed that during flow, people typically experience deep enjoyment, creativity, and a total involvement in life.

Flow is a state of consciousness. But it's easier said than done. Setting intentions and keeping a clear focus is key, as well as consciously choosing what not to do. Minimizing room for distractions and procrastination. Making sure you have space in your head versus always running around from meeting to meeting, chasing after one deadline to the next.

Being fully present in what you are doing right now will enable your creative juices and new ideas to flow.

One of the best and most inspiring examples of someone who truly understands and implements this concept of joy in his life and work is probably Richard Branson.

Branson originally started Virgin Records as a side project as part of *Student*, a magazine he was working on. It's worth noting that *Student* magazine was his first business, which he started at age 16 when he left school. According to Branson, "The magazine was created to provide an alternative to the stale publications and school magazines of the day." But a side project of that magazine was to sell mail-order records by running adverts for them in the magazine. They were all very passionate about music, so doing that on top of the work they already had, didn't feel like a heavy burden. Branson notes very clearly that, without passion, it is impossible to be successful at what you do. To quote Branson: "If you do what you love and love what you do, you're more likely to be successful."

Case study: The joys of joy

An interview with John Tanner, general manager of Chase Design Group, Los Angeles

I had the pleasure and honour of working with John Tanner for several years while we were both still living in New York. And even though the pressures in branding agency life can get pretty intense at times, one of the key things I always noticed when working with John was that he had this glow – a vibrant energy that literally lit up the room when he entered. Not to mention the amount of work he was able to pull off in a day. Most importantly, what struck me was how he always managed to motivate and inspire those around him to also have his can-do mentality and positive attitude. It was a no-brainer that he would be the perfect person to interview for the chapter on joy.

My interview with John, or Tanner as I always call him, was over the phone, in the middle of winter. As I was staring at a pack of snow outside my office, it was clearly much more pleasant in sunny California, where Tanner is based. He picked up the phone with his always-cheerful "Helloo?" A hello that stretches out the 'o' with a question mark at the end, which always puts a big smile on my face.

John, can you please tell us a little bit about your background and how you ended up where you are now?

When I was young I was already drawn to the creative field. I was always into art and drawing, and at age 11 I was taking adult art classes. I responded the most to creativity and art. In college I had the dream of ending up in the advertising business. I studied both art and business. That led me to where I am today, in the design world.

Currently, I'm the general manager at Chase Design Group. We have offices in LA and New York. What's key in my position is to make sure we have the right talent in the right seat. And because we are growing, we have been focused on hiring new talent. I'm also tasked with making sure we have the right mix of clients. In the end, your list of clients should be like a stock portfolio, and you want to ensure you have the right blend of different types of businesses and sectors.

What about your personal life and interests?

I love to travel and to experience the world, seeing what's out there. I have a long bucket list of places I want to visit, and keep crossing each one off my list. That couples nicely with my passion for design and architecture. I read design books about noted architects like someone else may read fiction. Renovating my house has also been a two-year passion. It's a project where I can channel my creative energies in home and landscape design.

What does leadership mean to you?

Leadership to me is really about creating the right environment for great things to happen. This is particularly important in the creative field. Creative people are usually highly emotional beings, so having the right environment is crucial. I believe in creating a positive environment where people can flourish.

Leadership is also about creating the right vision. Getting to a vision is a process with lots of stakeholders. It's an iterative and collaborative process. It's important to incorporate what people bring to the table, so the vision should be organic.

A good leader is also someone who stays positive and who doesn't let people down, but pushes and nudges them in the right direction.

I've worked with managers who were able to motivate people almost effortlessly. And you really are proud to work for someone like that. They were first and foremost very positive. When you stay positive, it's almost like nothing can stop you. The way you look at the world really impacts the reality around you. The opposite is true when someone is on a downer. It's like being on a boat and the captain jumps off when a big storm hits. You can't rally the troops that way.

How would you define awareness?

Awareness can be described almost like a sixth sense and the core of it is about listening versus talking. It's about understanding both the verbal and non-verbal cues around you. Being able to read people. It's about having awareness of your environment. It could be the market place, the clients, or the people you work with.

You have to be in a position to be receptive though, to be able to really listen and read between the lines. If you are caught up in your own world, you can't do that. It's about being centred and comfortable with who you are.

If you are panicking, you are not picking up on awareness because you are in your own world, so it's much more challenging. There are so many distractions. You really have to be quiet. That's also what meditation teaches you. It's about listening to your self.

What does joy mean to you?

Joy is the internal happiness that puts a smile on your face. When you are joyful you exude positivity and happiness, so it's also contagious.

How do you incorporate it in your personal life and work?

It's about picking up your bootstraps and going. When things are tough, it's thinking: how do we reframe this, is there a bright side to this, or how can we overcome it? It's not looking too deeply into the negative. It's about focusing on the things we can fix to make things better. So say you come out of a bad meeting, you really just have to laugh at it, find the humour in it, and look at the positive. It's being a little Teflon, as I call it. Not letting the bad stuff get to you too much. Don't let it stick. Some things may suck, and they will, but I have 20 other things I have going for me right now. So shift your focus on what is right. It's an attitude mostly, an attitude of looking on the bright side of life. That's what my parents instilled in me. I really feel that having a good upbringing is a huge asset; there is an inherent perception that you have naturally when you grow up learning to look at the positives.

How do you incorporate it in your work?

I think joy in the workplace comes down to collaboration. It's fostering this notion of collaboration and staying positive. At my current company we always say that nobody has a bad idea. We can all comment on the work we are doing. And it's OK to make comments. We are in this together.

Having fun and having that sense of camaraderie is key. It's good to have fun at the office, because it keeps morale high and keeps people motivated. Do things with colleagues like going out for drinks, or having excursions, or having a picnic in the park. It's very important to do those things, because it changes the energy in a group dynamic. Create an environment where that is the norm, so it's not only you as the leader that initiates it, but everyone.

Do you have any other thoughts on this topic?

In the end, happiness is what drives people. People want to be happy. You work because you need to survive, that's the functional part of working. But the emotional part is the happy part. You want to work to be happy. If we can inject happiness it makes work and life, which are completely intertwined, much more fulfilling.

Chapter 8:
Gratitude

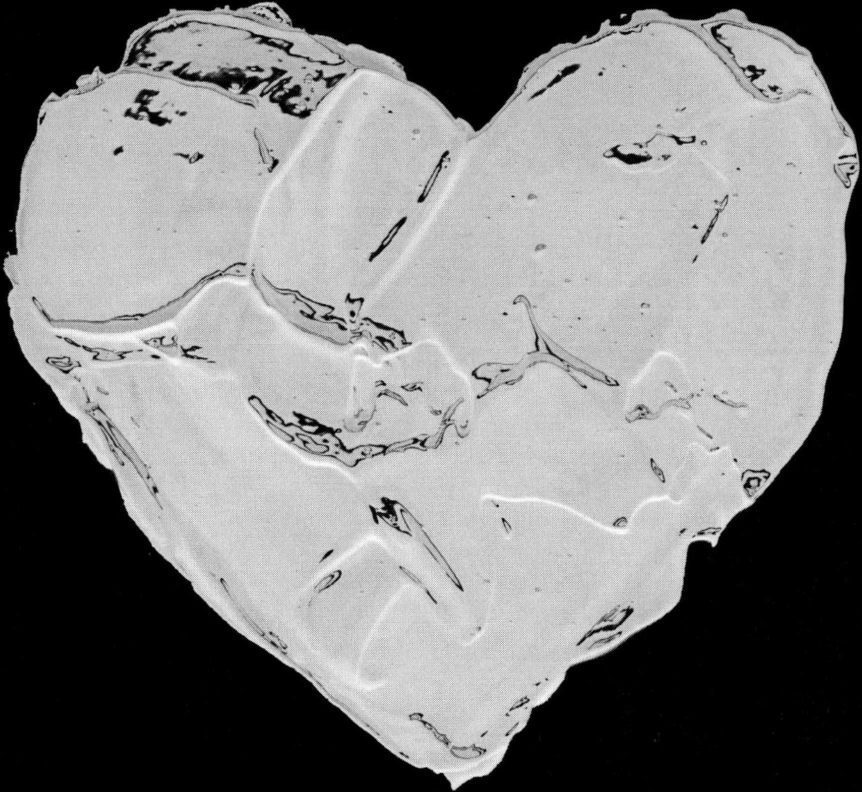

"If the only prayer you ever say in your life is thank you, it will be enough."

Meister Eckhart, theologian and philosopher

Gratitude is good for you. Before you think I'm being overly simplistic or even evangelical, it would be worthwhile to look at all the scientific research and results that confirm this statement.

Gratitude is not only good for you, but also for the people around you. It is one of the most important and beautiful things in life. It involves acknowledging and celebrating all the good that is present in your life. And there is more good than we often realize.

Research across the globe has shown the immense benefits of gratitude. These benefits extend to your personality, your emotional wellbeing, your social interactions, your health, your career, basically your whole life.

If you want to gain deeper levels of awareness, focus on gratitude. If you want to be a better leader, focus on gratitude. If you want to lead a happier life, focus on gratitude.

I cannot stress this enough.

Gratitude is where it all comes together.

On an emotional level, being grateful makes you feel rich beyond words. It makes you less envious of what other people have because you are focusing on yourself in a very positive way.

A great example of this is one of my former employers. He was leading a team of ten people and, every Christmas, he would invite everyone, including their partners, for a home-cooked dinner. This was not just any kind of dinner, mind you. A full-blown six-course meal, with wine pairings and the best conversation you can imagine. Obviously this made us all feel extremely valued and appreciated, especially because you could see how genuine the intentions were behind this beautiful gesture. But what I found even more remarkable about these dinners was that I could see the effect it had on him. You could see the sparkle in his eyes as he was presenting and serving each new dish. Whenever we would thank him for the beautiful food and all the effort he and his wife had put into it, he responded by saying, "It is nothing compared to all the hard work and energy you all put into the office day after day, so I thank you." By showing his gratitude to us in such a profound way every year, we would be inspired and motivated to work even harder back in the office.

Gratitude makes you less self-centred and gives you a more optimistic outlook on life. It even helps with building your self-esteem. Whenever you are down or nervous about a certain task at hand, just list the things you are grateful for regarding yourself. It can be as simple as saying "I like my smile". Or "I like how I am able to make people feel heard". Once you take time, just for a few minutes to do this, you will notice that those negative feelings you might have had will slowly subside.

You will notice that once you start practising gratitude more frequently, your relationships will deepen and you will be a kinder person overall. And as Lao Tzu, the ancient Chinese philosopher and writer said: "Kindness in words creates confidence. Kindness in thinking creates profoundness. Kindness in giving creates love."

Health-wise, you will notice that you will sleep better, believe it or not, have more energy, and even have a better immune system.

So practically speaking, how can we be more grateful when the world is rushing by?

Again, it all starts with awareness. Having awareness for all the things in your life that are worth being grateful for. And it really starts and ends with the small things.

The mere fact that you have a roof over your head and warm water running already puts you in the group of very privileged people in the world. And no matter what is going on in your day, gratitude allows you to focus on what you have versus what you are lacking.

One of the things I've learned during my 15 years in the business world is that what you focus your energy on will grow. So when you focus on gratitude, you focus on what's right in your life. And that focus makes the negativity that might be present in your life become smaller and smaller, and likewise expand the things you are grateful for.

Especially in the realm of leadership, gratitude makes you become less self-centred. Gratitude will force you to look at the people around you and give your attention to what they are doing well. This will always be noticed by those people, who will start feeling more appreciated, which in turn increases loyalty as well as productivity.

Perhaps the most amazing part about gratitude is its double-layered effect. As I mentioned earlier, when you express your gratitude to someone else, you feel good yourself as well.

Gratitude is important for organizations' performance, and a good example is one of the most successful hotel chains in the world: Marriott. (Source: Gallagher, Leigh. "Why employees love staying at Marriott", Fortune.com, March 5, 2015. <http://fortune.com/2015/03/05/employees-loyalty-marriott/>)

Every year, Marriott scores exceptionally high on employee satisfaction. Gratitude has proven to be a cornerstone in the company's success in keeping employees loyal. The company culture focuses on 'giving back' and this has become the norm throughout the company as a way for colleagues to deal with one another.

Marriott employees often use the word 'family' when they speak about their work environment. The company's track record of employee employment periods is impressive to say the least, with an average tenure for a hotel manager being 25 years. A figure that is very high, especially when compared with other hotel chains. More than 10,000 people have been with the company for over 20 years. It comes as no big surprise to hear that Marriott has been on Fortune's "Best Companies to Work For" list for more than 15 years.

So what is Marriott doing that makes it achieve such impressive numbers?

It gives back to its employees, and shows its sincere gratitude for the hard work people are putting in.

Some examples of employee benefits include childcare for working parents, a gym, a dry cleaning service, preferred parking for hybrid cars, substantial discounts for family and friends on room rates, to name just a few. When an employee has been with the company for 25 years or more, they become eligible for the Quarter Century Club, which means they get free weekend hotel stays for life.

But it's not just about what is given in terms of monetary value to employees – as in, it's not only about the tangibles. There are also the intangibles, which might actually even be more important. For example, every shift starts with a 15-minute stand-up meeting, to get pumped up for work. Each hotel can give their own swing to these meetings, but they are known to include stretching, music, and dancing. A sense of community and camaraderie is definitely created this way.

Once a year, every year, there is a big company-wide Awards of Excellence event. It's a very chic ceremony that recognizes and awards employees from all over the world. Employees get nominated and are flown in for the event, which is usually attended by about 800 workers and the entire executive team.

Marriot employees love the fact that if you work hard and are good at what you do, you truly do get rewarded and can grow a career based on merit. Stories of top executives, who started out at the bottom of the food chain, are inspiring to say the least.

It is clear from the above examples that giving back is taken quite seriously at Marriot and, very importantly, it shows how employees respond to that, which in turn benefits Marriott.

The beauty of gratitude is that it instantly gives a reward not only to the person you are thanking, but actually to the person who is extending his or her gratitude.

When we spoke about joy in the previous chapter, one of the key ways to get to joy was by looking for and acknowledging all the good things currently around you.

Gratitude is not only to be extended to people around you. You can be grateful within yourself for all the good in your life. The shift it brings in you will also benefit the people around you.

Gratitude is a way of being, which is truly all-encompassing.

Case study: Gratitude

An interview with Sarah Miller, assistant dean

It's not by chance that the last chapter in this book is about gratitude. Everything comes together in gratitude. For this chapter I have the pleasure and honour to interview Sarah Miller, who is one of those people with a beautiful but rare combination of strength and kindness about her. I was thrilled when she agreed to give me her thoughts on the concept of leadership and gratitude.

When I called Sarah for the interview, she was having a brisk walk outside. It was Sunday afternoon and she was taking some fresh air for the interview. I always love talking to Sarah as she is a great communicator and knows how to get straight to the point.

Sarah, can you please tell us a little bit about your background and how you ended up where you are now?

I started my career as a middle school teacher. I was teaching mathematics and science in a poor urban area in California. I absolutely loved it, and realized I could be a teacher forever. Then I went on to graduate school to see if I liked teaching at a higher level as well. I got my PhD in engineering at Yale. I also became a vice principal at the schools where I was volunteering. I wanted to do work focused on access and equity – so that everyone who wants to do science, can do science. That's how I ended up at the university I am now. When the opportunity came up to be the assistant dean for inclusive excellence, I accepted and my husband and I decided to move state for the job. I love every aspect of this amazing role. It says so much about the school that there is a role like this. It speaks to how important equity and inclusion is.

My key responsibility is to help students that have traditionally been underrepresented to get equal opportunities, and we do a lot on retention initiatives.

What does leadership mean to you?

There are all kinds of leaders. I've worked for people that instil fear, and that is how they drive or scare people to deliver. Then there are leaders who instil inspiration. I think, like most people, I prefer the latter. I try to be that person, recognizing the wonderful aspects that each of my team members brings to their job. I think the job of a leader is to bring out people's strengths and help them be the best they can be.

How would you define awareness?

Awareness to me has a couple of levels. First of all there is self-awareness. Awareness of who you are, and how others perceive you. To be that leader that inspires you to want to be perceived appropriately.

Then there is the awareness of how well you notice others. These can be tangible things but also less tangible. For example, when someone is acting a little bit differently or someone's behaviour is changing. If you are a leader in a team you need to be aware of the intangibles.

Awareness becomes important when there are successes to be celebrated, making sure that proper acknowledgment is given where it's due. It is also important to be aware when there are problems or challenges. Awareness as a leader is about knowing when to issue congratulations and when damage control is in order.

How do you incorporate awareness in your role as a leader?

One thing I do is I try to be aware and have a pulse on the team. There are ten of us and we have a group meeting every week. If I feel something isn't right, I try to take the time to figure out what that is. Often it's about following up with a specific person. I meet with everyone once a week. I do that so everyone has the space to have a thought partner and air any discontent they might have.

What does gratitude mean to you?

Gratitude is one of the most important things. I like to be surrounded by grateful people, both in my personal and professional life. What it means to me is acknowledging and celebrating people, for little things as well as the big things. The little things can be the most important. I try to do that by being very vocal about giving credit where credit should be given. I try to take the time to find quiet space to acknowledge hard work. For example, I try to write everyone a genuine note every couple of months, thanking them for the big and little contributions, and sacrifices they've made. Also, any time I see a call for nomination, I make an effort to nominate someone from my team who I think is deserving.

Most importantly, I think gratitude is about being humble. As I was thinking about gratitude, the word humble kept coming to my mind. I think that really is the core of it. Knowing and acknowledging that as a leader you are merely a part of the team. It is the team that really delivers – so many people are working hard on things.

What have been the effects of practising gratitude at work for you?

I think it shows in staff retention. I really like working with the people I work with and, so far, they've stuck around and performed well. I also think the people that work on the kind of things we work on are intrinsically kind and interesting people.

There is one final key thing to note about gratitude. Like many things that are good to do, gratitude has this effect of making you feel better about yourself. When you express gratitude that is genuine, it not only makes the person you are expressing your gratitude to feel better, but it also makes you feel better.

Tying it all together

some final thoughts

In essence, the key to being a better leader and a better person is to be aware. Learn to be your true self. Learn to *BE*.

The concepts we've looked at throughout this book can help you on that path to reaching deeper levels of awareness. Each are very powerful on their own, but what makes them even more powerful is when you combine them and practise them as a beautiful mix in your daily encounters with the people around you, as well as with yourself.

Intuition: The art of being still and connecting to your inner wisdom, without the need for conscious reasoning.

The North Star: The art of having a personal vision, driven by your heart's purpose as the foundation for your intentions, thoughts, and actions accordingly.

Surrender: The art of practising acceptance for what is; knowing when to let go of control, and to have trust on a deeper level.

I Am You: The art of empathy and compassion by realizing that we are all in this together and connected on a deeper level.

Vulnerability: The art of having the courage to truly be and show ourselves to others, and knowing we are worthy no matter what.

Insanity: The art of looking at the world with a fresh pair of eyes and daring to challenge the prevailing norms by carving out your own path.

Joy: The art of living life from a place of joy and light-heartedness by focusing on what you have and what you can contribute.

Gratitude: The art of being humble and looking at life through the lens of gratitude and appreciation.

An introduction to **Bahriye Goren-Gulek**

Bahriye Goren-Gulek is a brand strategy expert with 15 years of global experience, both on client side with Unilever and on agency side where she has consulted world class multinationals across the globe. As the former Executive Director Innovation and Strategy at Wallace Church & Co., an award winning branding agency in New York, she has worked with the most talented creative and brand leaders. She is a university lecturer at the graduate and undergraduate level at business schools in New York, Colorado, Singapore and Taiwan. She lives with her husband, son and their dog in Boulder, Colorado.